W9-AZL-546

MICHELE L. FLEURY

WHAT
THEY DON'T
TEACH YOU
IN BUSINESS
SCHOOL

REAL-WORLD SALES AND SERVICE SKILLS YOU NEED TO WIN AND WOW CLIENTS!

DEDICATION

To my parents, who sacrificed so much for their children, and who instilled the confidence in us to believe we could achieve whatever we wanted to achieve in life. Rest in peace, Mom; I wish you were here with us to see the launch of this book, but I know you are looking down on me and enjoying this moment from heaven.

To my husband, Alan, who constantly supports me in the pursuit of my dreams. Thank you for your endless encouragement and for always putting up with me! I love you!

To all my clients throughout my career, who have inspired me to write this book. Without you, this book would definitely not have been possible!

DOWNLOAD THE PRINTABLE COMPANION WORKBOOK FREE!

As a thank you for purchasing my book, I'd like to give you my Companion Workbook completely FREE!

Download the workbook here:

https://whattheydontteachyouinbusinessschool.lpages.co/freeworkbook/

CONTENTS

INTRODUCTION

So you've already started a business, you're incredibly talented with a creative skill, people keep telling you that your work is wonderful or that your business idea is great—but you can't seem to get good customers and keep them. Maybe you get the client the first time, but they never come back to your business again, and no one is referring other people to you. Perhaps you've started a small company, but you have no business experience or training, and you have no idea how to sell, service, or communicate with customers. Sound familiar? If so, this book is for you.

I'm going to solve this problem for you by illustrating a few simple communication, sales, and customer service techniques that you can immediately implement in your business. In this book, you will learn "tried and true" tactics, not "pie in the sky" ideas that are so broad they leave you wondering what to do next.

Throughout my career over the last 25 years, I've consistently worked directly with clients and customers. My positions in various industries in sales, business development, account management, and client service have equipped me with a wealth of knowledge on how to acquire clients and keep them coming back for more. I worked for large corporations for years and have been through so many sales and service training courses I can't even count them all. When I started my own small business, I quickly realized there are many people who want to start a business or do start a business, but they have absolutely no idea how to work with clients or how to turn those clients into satisfied customers.

The tips and tricks I'll show you in this book represent a lifetime of helpful hints and specific tactics I've used to attract, engage, sign, and satisfy clients for decades in both big businesses and small. When you start your own small business, you'll find many companies that can tell you how to set up a website, how to use social media accounts, and how to fund your company, but no one tells you the most important thing that will keep your business going: how do I win and keep satisfied customers? What do I say once they want to meet with me about my product or service? How do I work through issues with customers or avoid tough issues altogether?

Not only do I have more than two decades of experience selling and managing clients, but I've also learned from my mistakes along the way, so these techniques work. For example, I started a video production business with my husband several years ago, producing various types of videos for consumers and businesses, but I knew nothing about the video production field or the industry before starting our business. In just a few short years, our business became an award-winning, top-rated wedding video production company in the New England market, and the awards we won were based completely on our positive client reviews. Most companies in our industry get a sentence or two on a review site from their clients, but we've had paragraphs (even pages!) written by clients, all raving about their experiences with us!

Using my sales and service techniques will not just improve your relationships with your clients, but will keep them coming back to your business again and again. They'll send their friends your way, too! I promise you'll not only get more customers, but you'll get better reviews and glowing testimonials from them.

For the purposes of this book, I'm assuming that if you have your own business, then you already have a website and social media accounts in place, that your business is already essentially set up, and that you already have customers coming to your place of business. The purpose of this book is to help you improve your sales and customer service with those potential and existing customers.

So what are you waiting for? Don't be the person with a great business idea who fails because you can't keep your customers happy. Don't be the business owner who loses customers but can't figure out why. Don't be the person who is the best or the most talented at what you do, but who keeps losing to the competition. Without customers, you've got nothing—so make them your first priority.

Knowing how to talk to your clients, how to present and sell to them, and how to give them first-rate service are the keys to success for any small business. Each chapter in this book will help you have better meetings with your clients, improve communication with your customers and prospects, earn trust from your clients, and ultimately obtain more business, more referrals, and more positive reviews. Keep reading, and your customers will LOVE you!

Note: Throughout the book, I've used "client" and "customer" interchangeably, as well as "he" and "she."

CHAPTER 1

BACK TO BASICS

"Success is neither magical nor mysterious. Success is the natural consequence of consistently applying the basic fundamentals."
—Jim Rohn, entrepreneur, author, and speaker

"Customer service shouldn't just be a department, it should be the entire company."
—Tony Hsieh, internet entrepreneur and venture capitalist

"Back to basics" means going back to the fundamental principles of how humans should interact. You may not initially think these have to be taught, but time and time again, I've found there are so many basic fundamentals that business owners, sales people, account managers, and employees at *all* levels are simply not working into their communications with clients. Much of what my clients appreciate most about me stems from basic, easy-to-implement techniques that show how much my company cares about them.

What kinds of "basics" am I talking about? For starters, practicing good old-fashioned ethics, honesty, and manners. Next, remembering and using your clients' names, getting back to people in a timely manner, having a sense of urgency, and going above and beyond. And last, but certainly not least: doing what you say you're going to do, *when* you say you're going to do it!

When I start talking about these fundamental principles, I think of Robert Fulghum's book, *All I Really Need to Know I Learned in Kindergarten*. Let's start with his "basics," as outlined in his book, to give you an idea of where I'm going with this concept.

These are the things I learned (in Kindergarten):

1. Share everything.
2. Play fair.
3. Don't hit people.
4. Put things back where you found them.
5. CLEAN UP YOUR OWN MESS.

6. Don't take things that aren't yours.

7. Say you're **SORRY** when you **HURT** somebody.

8. Wash your hands before you eat.

9. Flush.

10. Warm cookies and cold milk are good for you.

11. Live a balanced life—learn some and drink some and draw some and paint some and sing and dance and play and work every day some.

12. Take a nap every afternoon.

13. When you go out into the world, watch out for traffic, hold hands, and stick together.

14. Be aware of wonder. Remember the little seed in the Styrofoam cup: The roots go down and the plant goes up and nobody really knows how or why, but we are all like that.

15. Goldfish and hamster and white mice and even the little seed in the Styrofoam cup—they all die. So do we.

16. And then remember the Dick-and-Jane books and the first word you learned—the biggest word of all—LOOK.

—Fulghum, Robert. *All I Really Need to Know I Learned in Kindergarten: Uncommon Thoughts on Common Things.* New York: Villard Books, 1988.

Simple rules, right? These are extremely basic fundamentals that you learned when you were a young child, and Fulghum has adopted them as a "personal statement of belief," a life credo. Fulghum tells us he already *knows* most of what he needs to know to live a meaningful life. And he's known it since Kindergarten! Living it, though? As Fulghum says, "well, that's another matter."

It's that way with communication, too—the principles in this chapter are things you might think most people already know, or you may believe that most people are already doing these things with their clients. The truth is, that's not the case at all, and we often need a friendly reminder of the "basics"—just as Fulghum reminded us to "share," to "play fair," and to "say you're sorry when you hurt somebody."

Remember, it's all about the client, *not* about you. Remember what you learned in Kindergarten. Remember the fundamentals in life, as a start, and it will take you a very long way.

So let's talk about my own list of "basics," as it relates to communication:

1. Make ethics your first priority.

What do I mean by ethics? Honesty, doing the right thing, morals, and treating people the way you want to be treated. When it comes down to it, people want to do business with people they trust: nice, reasonable, understanding people. If you treat people the way you treat your friends, they can't help but want to work with you. When you're in the midst of a difficult client situation, ask yourself: What would Mom do? What would you say if it were your best friend on the other end of the phone or on the other side of the counter?

Here's an example. Let's say you hear from a client who was supposed to be meeting with you to book your services and make his first payment (and you really need the money, by the way). The client cancels at the last minute due to a death in the family, or a sick relative he needs to visit in the hospital. What is the very first thing you should do? No matter how tempting it is to ask him to mail in his payment to you, you *must* forget about the money for now.

Acknowledge the death or sick relative *first*, and give the client your condolences or good wishes. Don't even try to reschedule the appointment—he clearly has other things on his mind. Ask if there is anything you can do to help (and mean it!). Tell him to get back in touch with you when he is "settled" again, and then he can worry about rescheduling with you. If you are holding a date of service for the client, continue to hold the date until you hear back from him. It's the right thing to do, and the circumstances are obviously beyond his control. You can always get back in touch with the client at a later date to reschedule if you haven't heard back from him within a reasonable timeframe. If you're worried that this illness is a bogus excuse and he is "blowing you off," you'll know that soon enough; give people the benefit of the doubt the first time.

To see first-hand what I mean, read what a client wrote about my husband and me in an online review about our business. Make note of what stood out *most* to this client after the project was finished:

> When I think of our experience of having MPD Video capture our wedding day the first word that comes to mind is 'excellence'! Truly, there is not much more one has to say. From day one with our initial contact until we obtained our most anticipated final copy, there is nothing I would change, and nothing more I could have asked for. We so greatly appreciated the quality and service that was provided that both my husband and I decided to share

our thoughts in a review. Both Michele and Alan were incredibly professional, and went above and beyond on more than one occasion in order to meet my husband's and my needs. **What stands out most for me, though, is the warmth, patience, and understanding that they provided following an unexpected death in our family right before the wedding took place.** They were a blessing to us, and so it is without any reservation that I whole-heartedly recommend this team for your special day or any other videography needs.

Believe me, little things always go a long way. Do the right thing. Be real, be nice, be flexible, be honest, and if you make a mistake (you will at some point—we all do!), just own up and fix it.

2. Use basic manners.

If your parents or grandparents didn't teach you basic manners as a child, you need to learn them now:

Use the words *please, thank you,* and *my apologies.* You should use one of these words or phrases in almost every email, phone, or text conversation with your clients. If you are not using *please* and *thank you,* you have a problem. Clients always need to be thanked for their time, their business, their reviews, for getting back to you with info you requested, and for choosing your company over your competition. Add these simple words to your vocabulary immediately.

After saying hello in an email, I typically insert phrases like *thank you for your email*, *thank you for your inquiry about our services*, or *thank you for getting in touch*, as a starting sentence in my email. As a standard practice, I also close each email by writing *thank you* as either a final phrase in my email, or prior to my email signature. I call this the "bookend" approach: always start positively and end positively, like "bookends" on your message.

Please can also easily be inserted into most communications with your clients. Simply adding the word *please* into a question such as "Can you let me know?" will softly change the tone of your message to your client.

Phrases like *my apologies* or *my sincerest apologies* can also be inserted into your messages when the client is upset, when he misunderstands what you wrote or said, or when you are working through the resolution of an issue with him.

Here's an example of one of my own emails to a client, to

demonstrate the use of basic manners:

Hi Judy,

Thank you for your inquiry about our professional videography services. We'd be happy to help you with video for your upcoming dance recital.

I'm so glad to hear that Mary at ABC Studio recommended that you contact us. I'll be sure to thank her for sending you our way! My apologies on the delay in getting back to you -- we were out filming events over the weekend, so I'm responding to all of my email messages today.

We're booked on Sat., June 17th, but we do have availability for your show on Sun., June 18th, 2017. What time and where will your performance be held?

Also, if you could please let me know how many students will be participating in the performance, and the estimated length/run-time of the show, that would be helpful for pricing purposes as well.

I'd be glad to call you at a convenient time to go over details and to discuss how the process works, but I wanted to at least get back to your initial inquiry today so you'd know that we do have availability on your show date.

Are you available tomorrow or Wednesday between 3:00 and 5:00 pm to chat briefly by phone?

All of my contact info is listed below for your reference. I look forward to hearing back from you and to the opportunity to work with XYZ Dance Studio!
Thank you again,
Michele Fleury

Notice the use of *please*, *thank you*, and *my apologies* in the above email, my very first communication with the client.

Another element of basic manners: turn the cell phone and computer off during meetings. If you're meeting with a client or talking with a client on the phone, you need to give him your full attention. You may not think this is important, but consider how annoying it is when you're explaining something important on the phone and all you hear is the typing of keys on the keyboard in the background! You can clearly tell the person on the other end of the phone is not listening to you.

If you tell the client up front that you want to take some notes from your meeting on the computer, that's perfectly fine, but if not, don't do it. The same goes for the cell phone—it's very rude to see someone looking down at his phone when you're trying to have a serious conversation with him. Give the client your full attention. If you absolutely have to leave the phone on because you're expecting a call about the birth of your first child or your dad is coming out of surgery, tell that to the client up front, and do NOT answer the phone unless it is that emergency call coming through.

3. Use your client's name, and use it correctly.

I'll never forget the time I went shopping with my husband for a new suit coat (I've omitted the name of the men's clothing store to protect the guilty). The sales clerk asked my husband his name, so he responded, "Hi, I'm Alan." The clerk continued to use my husband's name as he offered him several clothing options throughout the store. Each time he reached a new option that he wanted my husband to consider, he said, "Al!," "Hey, Al!," or "Look at this, Al!" My husband's name, as he had clearly said, is *Alan*, not Al. If he had wanted to be called Al, he would have said so when he introduced himself.

And talk about overuse of my husband's name! It was as if this clerk had taken a sales course and the instructor had told the class to use the customer's name in every other sentence. Bottom line, I couldn't wait to get out of the store—and we didn't buy anything. This mistake is the equivalent of calling me "Shelly"—my name is Michele, and never in my life have I been called "Shelly" by anyone. Call people what they want to be called, and if the client says her name is "Elizabeth," don't take the liberty of calling her "Beth" or "Liz."

The proper use of names also applies to written communications. Many people misspell my name as "Michelle" instead of the correct "Michele." Those who pay attention to detail and spell my name correctly in written messages automatically get bonus points from me. It only takes an extra minute to double-check the spelling of the client's name before hitting send, but it will definitely go a long way with your clients if you take the time to spell their names correctly.

4. Respond promptly.

Responding promptly does not mean that whenever you get an inquiry from your website or a call from a client, you need to reply within minutes. Your time is valuable and you need to prioritize your tasks and your client communications each day. However, if someone wants information on your products or services, you should establish a general timeframe in which you respond to all new inquiries.

What is a reasonable timeframe? Perhaps you could set aside a time of day to respond to all voicemail messages, or pick a specific timeframe and stick to it (i.e. respond on the same day as the initial inquiry, or within 24 hours from receipt of initial inquiry).

Also, consider how quickly your business *needs* to respond. I find that my potential clients frequently say, "Thank you so much for your quick response"—which tells me I'm often responding quicker than my competition, even when I don't think I'm responding as quickly as I should!

Remember, responding to an inquiry doesn't mean you have to answer all the potential client's questions right away, but at least let the client know you've received the message by responding within a reasonable period of time and requesting a time to meet or talk further. Try telling him when you can dedicate a certain amount of time to talk, or briefly explain that you are unavailable at that time, but ask him for a good time to answer his questions. If applicable to your business, you can ask the client for additional information or details you might need before you can answer his specific questions, or before you can give him a price for your product or service. This tactic will "buy" you some time with the client, since now he needs to respond to you before you can provide him with the information he requested. If customers at least know that you received their messages, they will immediately be more at ease.

Always remember, it's about the client; it's not about you. If you truly make the client feel as if his needs are important and his project matters, you'll be amazed at the results.

5. Be excited and have a sense of urgency.

If you're excited about your product or service, people can tell. If your enthusiasm is fake, people can tell. It really doesn't take much to be perceived as "better" than your competition if you're truly excited about what you're doing! If someone contacts you to work an event next year, you don't need to treat it with as much of a sense of urgency as someone who calls you to work an event next week, but you still need to be excited about it! Grab a cup of coffee before the client meeting and "turn it on." If you want to take a nap after the meeting because you happen to have a terrible cold that day, you can do that later, but you must "turn it on" for the client meeting. Smile, have energy, make eye contact, pay attention to what the client says, and be as excited as the client is. Have a sense of urgency about what the client needs and show excitement about each client's project!

I had a new client call me the other day, and after asking him several questions about his project, listening to his questions and answering them fully, and making him feel like his project mattered to me, he made a statement I'll never forget. He told me he had already called two or three other companies in my field, and he had felt like a "number." He said that every other company he spoke with made him feel as if the details of his event (his wedding day) didn't really matter to them. If they didn't book *his* wedding, they would just book someone else's. In other words, the video production companies I was competing against were "factories," churning through clients, treating a wedding as if it were just another date on the calendar.

Can you imagine? Your wedding day treated as if it's just another day? It's only one of the most important days in your life! Needless to say, we won the client by taking the time to answer all his questions, and by treating his event as it should be treated. The client truly felt that we would handle his wedding day like the unique and incredibly important day it was.

6. Go above and beyond.

Going above and beyond does not have to mean spending huge amounts of money or making larger-than-life gestures. Little things really do go a long way. When I send out wedding videos to my clients, I often include a hand-written note in a pretty gift bag with some candy for the couple to enjoy while watching their wedding video. It's a small gesture and it doesn't cost a lot of money, but it's a personal touch that shows our clients we care. I can't tell you how many positive comments we've received about that thoughtful bag of candy! It's a simple idea, but it's an extra touch that shows we go above and beyond to make our clients feel special.

And last, but certainly not least:

7. Do what you say, when you say you're going to do it.

I talk a lot more about this in Chapter 6, but this one is so very important. Don't leave people hanging. If for some reason you can't do what you said you would do in the timeframe you promised, then contact the client on the day of the deadline (or earlier) and tell him why you haven't gotten back in touch yet, and then tell him when he'll actually have an answer from you. If you can't get back to the customer by Friday, don't say you'll provide an answer by Friday! Instead, ask the customer if the following Monday works, and if he says yes, then he'll be pleasantly surprised if you get back to him with an answer on Friday.

—

If you've started a business and your only goal is the money, and if treating people right is not part of your plan, you're going to have a very tough time as a business owner. Bottom line: treat others with respect and make them feel special. Be authentic. If your words and actions come from the heart, it will take you further than you could have ever imagined with your clients.

And remember, being "nice" does not have to mean being a pushover—kindness should not be mistaken for weakness. I definitely make sure my clients know that, and you can, too. If a client or a potential client crosses a certain line, or if that client tries to take advantage of me or my company, believe me, they'll realize immediately that I have the strength to push back. There is a huge difference between "kindness" and "weakness."

We've talked about the importance of ethics and basic manners, response time, using the client's name, urgency, and going above and beyond. But why does all of this matter? Why are these basic items and the way you communicate with your clients so important?

In today's technological world, good communication and stellar service are truly more crucial to your business than ever. We'll talk more about why in Chapter 2, but the words of Jeff Bezos, founder and CEO of Amazon.com, might help it make sense. Think about it this way:

"If you make customers unhappy in the physical world, they might tell 6 friends. If you make customers unhappy in the internet world, they might tell 6,000 people."
—Jeff Bezos

Ask yourself the following question before moving on to the next chapter:

What three "basics" can you start implementing in your client communications today?

CHAPTER 2

EFFECTIVE COMMUNICATION AND SETTING EXPECTATIONS—KEY ASPECTS OF CUSTOMER SERVICE

"Communication—the human connection—is the key to personal and career success."

—Paul J. Meyer, founder of the personal development industry

"The key is to set realistic customer expectations, and then not to just meet them, but to exceed them—preferably in unexpected and helpful ways."

—Richard Branson, business magnate, investor, philanthropist

Before we discuss the details of customer service, I'm first going to answer three questions you might have:

1. Why is good customer service so critical?

2. Why is effective communication such a key part of customer service?

3. Why is setting clear expectations such an important aspect of communication, and how can I set expectations with my clients and still have them end up happy, satisfied customers?

1. Why is good customer service so critical?

Bottom line: if you don't have satisfied customers, you eventually won't have a business. I am a true believer that if you don't treat clients well, poor service will catch up with you over time. Think about it this way:

Happy Customers = More Business and More Referrals
Unhappy Customers = No Business and No Referrals

Simple, right? Unfortunately, this concept is not so simple to everyone, but it applies to all types of businesses: restaurants, bakeries, consultants, photographers, wedding venues, event planners, retailers, and more. Many business owners either don't realize the ramifications of bad communication and bad service, or they just don't care. Why should *you* care?

In today's technological world, everything is posted online.

Between organizations like Yelp, Google reviews, the Better Business Bureau, and dozens of industry-specific review websites, a bad experience with you or your business can be posted to the entire world in a matter of seconds. It's extremely tough to recover from negative online posts, because you can't simply remove these posts from the internet. In many cases, the posts are etched into your online reputation forever.

A dissatisfied customer can say what she wants to online, and no one will ever know the "backstory" or what *really* happened. You can respond to these types of complaints either online or by contacting the customer directly, but the online complaints themselves can often never be removed—so it's important to resolve these situations well before the customer feels the need to take to the internet. Talk about an incentive to treat people well! Maintaining a positive online reputation should be one of your top goals. Keep this in mind when trying to decide how to communicate with an irate client, and before hitting "send" on that email when you are tempted to tell the client to "take a hike." Take a deep breath and think about it before you respond.

If a bad review isn't incentive enough for you, look at the flip side. What are the consequences of good service and good communication? Happy customers yield more customers through more referrals. Happy customers yield more positive reviews online. Happy customers result in more business and a positive reputation in your industry. If you communicate with your clients correctly and set expectations properly, you will have satisfied customers, and I'll show you how to achieve that goal throughout this book.

And remember, it's not just the customer on the other side of the counter or desk you need to satisfy. Indirect customers are important too.

What do I mean by "indirect customers"? Consider your vendors or suppliers. Do they like to do business with you? Do you treat them as if they're also your customers? Vendors, suppliers, employees, and other industry connections are all indirect customers who need to be included in your "customer" sphere. If your reputation in your industry is horrible and no one in the industry wants to work with you because you're abrasive, berating, unethical, or difficult to deal with, why in the world would anyone think you treat your customers any differently? Would you refer a friend to a businessperson with those qualities?

I constantly see businesses that want to blame their problems on the economy, the competition, being priced out of the industry, etc., but these are excuses. Think about how you are truly treating your customers as well as others who surround your business. People *will* pay more and *will* return to a business if they receive better service, a better product, or a better overall experience. That is, *if* they trust they'll be taken care of properly, and *if* they like and trust the people working with them.

2. Why is effective communication such a key part of customer service?

Here's an example of effective communication that will show you why it is such a critical part of customer service. There's a restaurant in my local area ("Jack's") that looks great on the outside. Jack's has a beautiful outdoor patio, a lovely indoor dining area, and looks classy and stylish. Yet every time I drive by the restaurant, no one is eating there! And this is in a small town where the restaurant choices are extremely limited. Whether it's a busy lunch hour or a Saturday night, I never see anyone there.

Recently, a new restaurant ("Jill's") opened up down the street from Jack's—and it's absolutely packed every weekend, at lunchtime, and anytime I drive by! The line of people to get in to Jill's is constantly out the door because of the stellar service, welcoming atmosphere, and excellent food. I've read the online reviews on Jack's and they are terrible, yet no one seems to pay attention to the complaints about the food or the service. Jill's, on the other hand, has a great rating online, and if they receive a less-than-stellar review, the manager writes back online, thanks the customer for the review, and asks him to get in touch with her personally so she can try to "make it right." What a difference in these two places and their approaches to customer service! I honestly expect Jack's to be out of business within a matter of months.

What's the moral of this story? If you're a restaurant owner and your customers are complaining about the food, but you're not doing anything to change it, you've got a real problem. If your customers are going across town to pack another restaurant every Saturday night instead of yours, you need to figure out why. Maybe you have no clue why nobody wants to eat at your restaurant on Saturday night, but you need to find that out quickly. How can you do that? Communicate with your customers! What do your customers truly think about the way your business has been treating them? Ask them what you need to do to become their favorite restaurant in town. Ask them how the service was, how the food was, what could be improved—and figure out a way to record that information.

Try leaving a short survey on the table for your customers to fill out quickly and anonymously, and ask them to submit it when they pay the bill. Ask three simple questions, and leave a space for comments. And don't just leave the survey on the table and hope they complete it; ask them verbally to please take a few minutes to fill out the survey. Then read the answers and honestly try to address the concerns. If Jack's simply cared enough to communicate with their customers and make some changes, they might not be on the verge of closing!

Also, look up your own business online and read the reviews that show up on Google. Is there a consistent theme in those reviews? If you don't know what you're doing wrong, you can't fix it. It's difficult and scary to ask your customers for feedback, but if you actually take the constructive or negative feedback and try to address it, you will put yourself and your business in a much better position. Everyone makes mistakes, but redeeming yourself by trying to correct those mistakes—and committing to not repeating them—will set you apart from your competition.

3. Why is setting clear expectations such an important aspect of communication? How can I set expectations with my clients and still have them end up happy, satisfied customers?

Setting clear expectations is one of the most important aspects of communication. Many business owners, however, choose not to set clear expectations, often because they are fearful their clients won't like the timeframe, price, or payment terms they require. In fact, the opposite is true—if you set clear expectations and explain the reasoning behind these important items up front, your clients will appreciate your honesty and you will gain agreement from your clients *before* investing time or money in their projects. No one likes surprises, especially surprises that involve bad news like higher pricing or longer completion timeframes than expected. In particular, no one likes surprises that could have been avoided altogether! Clients are often perfectly fine with waiting a bit longer than initially estimated for the final product—that is, if you don't avoid communication with them, and if they are given a reasonable explanation for the change.

Below, you're going to see an example of how communication of the same delivery timeframe in two similar types of businesses can result in two completely different online reviews. When you compare the reviews below, you'll see how the two businesses affected a client's perception of timeframe for delivery. My company's timeframe for delivery was basically the same as one of our competitor's, yet our review was glowing and positive, and the competitor's review was scathing and negative. Why? We communicated with the client and set clear expectations throughout the project.

First, I explain our timeframe for delivery up front to every client (along with the reasons why it takes that amount of time), and I get her commitment that she can live with our timeframe. I also put the timeframe in the contract—getting this agreement in writing is crucial! If the client is concerned about the timeframe, we talk about it and I try to be flexible, where possible. No, I can't simply go from delivering a full wedding video plus a highlights film that normally takes 12 weeks down to a two-week delivery schedule just because a particular client wants to have the video right away, but I *can* make reasonable adjustments based on the client's circumstances. Maybe the client has a sick grandparent who wants to see the wedding ceremony quickly because they are too ill to attend the wedding. Will I make an exception to the agreed-upon schedule and edit that client's ceremony first? Yes! I'll send the edited ceremony video to the client to show the grandparent—but I'll tell the client it's only a "rough-cut" edit of the ceremony, we'll agree on a clear timeframe for delivery of that particular piece of the video *only*, and I'll reserve the right to make changes to the final edit as needed.

Always look for a reasonable solution to a client's problem. If it were *your* grandmother or *your* wedding, what would you expect? Yes, of course I made an exception in the above case! But I came up with a reasonable solution and compromised based on the client's problem; I didn't agree to finish the entire wedding video weeks earlier than normal because I knew I couldn't deliver on that promise!

Take a look at the two online reviews below to see my point. The first one is about our business, posted by one of our clients. I've put positive feedback and specifics on delivery timeframe in bold print.

> I was referred to MPD Video Productions by my wedding DJ. We originally hadn't budgeted for a videographer and didn't think we had the money to pay for one. With my concerns in mind, when I talked to Michele on the phone she worked to customize a package that could fit within my limited budget, while still providing me full coverage of my special day. Michele & Alan have a lot of experience filming weddings, and I was completely at ease after our phone conversations that they had everything on their end taken care of. That is saying a lot, coming from a bride who had to plan the wedding from 700 miles away. They

were at our rehearsal the day before to meet us, observe a run-through of our ceremony, and go over the final details.

At our wedding, Michele and Alan used their two high-def cameras to capture multiple angles of all the special moments -- me walking down the aisle and my husband's reaction -- along with me and my husband getting ready separately, and coverage of our guests at cocktail hour while we went to take pictures with the bridal party.

Most importantly, not only is the work high-quality, but they have a very fast turn-around getting the videos back to you after the day is done. We had our highlights video and full videos within 3 months of our wedding. Our highlights video is posted online so we can easily share it with family and friends. The full-length video is split into chapters with the option also of watching the entire video at once. The footage is unbelievable; it feels like I get to go back in time and be a guest at my own wedding. The day goes by in a blur and reliving through pictures is not the same as hearing voices and re-watching special moments like our exchange of vows, first dance, and the dances with our parents.

If you want high-quality, personal, friendly, professional, affordable wedding videography in Massachusetts, then Michele and Alan of MPD Video Productions should be your first and only choice.

The following online review is about a competitor's business; I've put negative feedback and specifics on delivery timeframe in bold print.

After waiting a ridiculous 4 months to receive the video from my wedding, I was definitely unimpressed. We only wanted the ceremony taped so I thought we would get the video fairly quickly but boy was I wrong. When I finally received the video it looked like it was barely edited, the two angles it was shot from were terrible and the quality of the video was poor. They didn't even get a front view of me walking down the aisle and several minutes of footage are of an empty stage. The editing may have been worse than the footage itself. At one point in time someone stood up in front of the camera. Instead of moving the camera, or switching to the view of the other camera, our video contains nearly a full minute of the back of someone's head. I'm not kidding. We booked for a couple of hours of footage since they didn't have a ceremony only package so

I also thought there would be a little footage from cocktail hour or interviewing our guests. But no, nothing, it didn't seem like much for the amount of time they were there. My 10-year-old cousins could have gotten better footage and done the same editing work. **I strongly urge everyone to look elsewhere.**

I think you get the picture after reading these two completely different reviews. Wow! I would certainly not want to be the company that has to live with the second review! This terrible evaluation will likely be posted online forever, for the whole world to see. Both companies have a similar timeframe for delivery, but one client is thrilled and the other client is ripping mad. Clearly, the company in the second review did not discuss what would (or would not) be captured on video during the contracted timeframe, what would be involved in the editing process, the delivery timeframe, or what was most important to the client before the wedding day. It's all about communicating and establishing expectations ahead of time—if not, you're setting yourself up for unsatisfied or angry clients!

Here are some additional examples from my own business that can help you understand why it's so critical to set clear expectations.

- A business executive needed a video produced more quickly than I initially expected, because his department needed to show the video at the company's upcoming annual meeting as a part of their presentation.
- A professional speaker needed a promotional video produced in time for the launch of his new book.
- An entrepreneur needed us to complete video production work before the launch of his new website.

Each of these examples presents potential deviations in the schedule I discussed with each client before the project started—not after the client received the contract or after an unexpected situation arose. Can you imagine if I had failed to talk with my clients about delivery timeframe in these examples? If I hadn't asked the executive about expected completion timeframe and then set expectations accordingly, I would have been in deep trouble the week of his annual meeting!

If you wait to discuss these types of important issues (timeframe for delivery, payment terms, final deliverable, etc.) until the client receives the contract, you risk miscommunication or ignorance. Your client might not have read the part in the contract about the timeframe. What is he expecting in terms of delivery or completion timeframe? Always ask this question and discuss it with your client before starting the project! Again, you don't want your client to be surprised, but you are also protecting yourself by having this conversation.

If you don't have the delivery timeframe discussion with your client up front, you risk not charging the right amount for the project; you may end up losing money because you're scrambling to get the job done more quickly just to keep him happy. Think about it: if a client absolutely *needs* to have a typical two-week to three-week project done in one week, shouldn't you charge more for it? You'll likely have to work extra hours to finish it in time, or perhaps pay your employees overtime. You've also had to put off new clients, and there is a cost to that. If you don't understand the client's expected timeframe before beginning the project and you have to expedite delivery, that could translate into lost revenue and lost profit for your company. If you've discussed the timeframe upfront, the client may be completely willing to pay for an expedited timeframe.

Discussing the schedule before a project begins, and agreeing on what to do if unanticipated events occur, is crucial if you want to avoid unhappy clients. Don't wait because you feel it's the client's responsibility to read the contract. When's the last time *you* actually read every line of a contract you signed?

Communicate these important types of information up front. Delivery timeframe, payment terms, and what your final deliverable will include are all great examples of key items to discuss and agree on before the project begins.

One last point regarding setting expectations on timeframe: don't assume the client necessarily needs the job done by tomorrow. When discussing the project details with your client, simply ask your client if he has a particular timeframe in mind, or you can say something like:

- "I should be able to have this done by the end of this month. Does that work for you?"
- "Our typical timeframe for a project like this is about 4 to 6 weeks. Does that work for you?"

These types of questions will open the discussion about timeframe with your client. Get the client's buy-in to your timeframe. He will most certainly tell you if your projected timeframe doesn't work, and then you can discuss and agree upon a timeframe that's acceptable for both of you.

—

Now that you know why good customer service, effective communication, and setting expectations are so important, do you think you're ready for the first call or the first meeting with your client? You have your business set up, you have a website, you have pricing, you have a social media and marketing strategy, and clients are coming your way. Do you know what to do now?

In Chapter 3, we'll talk about what you need to do before that first client meeting, how to handle the meeting, what to talk about with the client, and more importantly, what questions to ask the client.

Before moving on to the next chapter, ask yourself this question:

What are three reasons to have a good service reputation in your business or industry? Alternatively, what are three consequences of bad service you want to avoid?

CHAPTER 3

YOU GOT THE CALL. NOW WHAT?

"Proper planning and preparation prevents poor performance."
—Stephen Keague, author and public speaker

"By failing to prepare, you are preparing to fail."
—Benjamin Franklin, American Founding Father and inventor

So you have a potential client interested in your product or services—great! But how do you handle the first meeting or call? Many small-business owners have absolutely no idea what to do at the first meeting, and many have no process or plan for that first client interaction. If you don't have a plan, you're doing yourself and your business a disservice.

What should your plan be? What types of research or preparation should you do in advance? What questions should you ask the client? There are several steps you need to take before and during your meeting with your soon-to-be customer.

1. Go back to basics.

Remember the fundamentals we talked about in Chapter 1? Rely on the basics of ethics, honesty, and basic manners. Make a mental note of the kinds of words you want to use in the meeting: *please, thank you*, and *my apologies*. Make a written and mental note of the names of the people who will be at the meeting, and use those names appropriately during the meeting. Think about how you'll show your enthusiasm and a sense of urgency. In what ways can you go above and beyond? Think about how you plan to set expectations properly so you respond to your client's requests in a reasonable period of time, and to ensure that you do what you say you're going to do, when you say you're going to do it. Reminding yourself of these basics *before* going into the meeting will set you off in the right direction.

2. Determine your goal for the call or meeting.

Your goal will depend on your product or service, and it will also depend on how long it typically takes to sell your goods or services. When I'm first working with a client, my goal is not necessarily for the client to commit to buying my services at the end of the first call, because it often takes several meetings or follow-up calls and emails to sell my services. Instead, my goal for the first client interaction is often to simply get to know the client and gather all the information I need. That way, I can put together pricing (or a proposal) by the time the call has ended.

Maybe your goal is simply to determine whether the potential client is a good "fit" for your business, because you can never be all things to all people. Not everyone is your ideal customer. (More about that later.)

Perhaps your goal might be to secure another meeting with the client to review your proposal or pricing, or to get a commitment from her to take the next step with your business (i.e., signing the contract, securing the first payment, etc.). Having an overall objective in mind and a clear goal for your client calls or meetings will help guide you in the direction you need to go with each particular client.

Now that you have a goal in mind for your meeting, what's next? Do you think you're ready to take the call or attend the meeting? No, wait—there's more!

3. Research and pre-plan.

What does research and pre-planning involve? Part of the process is thinking about and writing down your questions for the client in advance of the call or meeting. But pre-planning also means doing your research online. Use the internet to your advantage.

Just by doing a Google search, you can quickly learn a lot about a person: where she went to school, what she does for a living, what company she works for, and what interests she has. You can also learn about a company—its mission, management team, values, and upcoming events. You can effectively use all this information during your client meetings and conversations.

Let's take my wedding clients as an example. After I receive an inquiry through my website, I can often find the couple online by doing a Google search, which often leads to a wedding website containing details of their wedding day. The website will usually tell me the wedding venue, the timing of their day, how they met, their bridal party, and their proposal story. I can then look up the wedding venue (if I haven't worked there before) to learn about the location and to gather details about the site that I can use in my conversation with the client. The couple doesn't even know that I looked them up online (and I don't tell them—I don't want to look like a stalker!), but I can see what I have in common with them in advance. Perhaps we went to the same college, worked for similar companies or in similar fields in the past, or have a hobby in common. Now that I know these kinds of things, I can mention them during the conversation to establish rapport or to establish common ground.

For example, if I know the bride and I went to the same college in Boston, I may say something like:

"I noticed you picked a wedding venue in Boston . . . do you guys live there, or did you go to school there? Or is there some other connection to the city that made you want to get married there?"

Now remember, I already know the couple lives in Boston, or met at Boston College, from reading it online on their wedding website. Depending on how the client answers my question, I may continue by saying something like,

"I love Boston too—I went to school at Boston College and I lived in and around the city for many years after college."

The client's typical response is something like:

"Wow, I went to college there too! My fiancé and I met at Boston College!"

By carefully weaving this pre-researched fact about going to the same college into the conversation, I don't look like a stalker, but I do intentionally establish common ground with the client without her even knowing it! Now we have something in common that would probably have never come up in the conversation had I not done my research. The client feels more at ease and feels as if she already knows me because we have something in common.

Now that you've determined your goal for the meeting, done your research, and made a note of your questions (we'll go over those in a minute), you're ready to meet with your client.

4. Build rapport.

Once the client meeting or call starts, always build rapport and establish a relationship of trust before getting "down to business." Ask how the client is doing, how her day or week is going, and talk about items unrelated to business. If it's a Monday, ask how her weekend was, and truly listen to the answer. Your aim is to make the client feel comfortable, and you may even find out about more areas of commonality with her. If she is having a bad day, respond to that by letting her vent for a few minutes, and respond by honestly telling her you hope her day gets better! If meeting face to face, chat with her while offering her a glass of water, a cup of coffee, or a snack.

5. Set the agenda and get your client's agreement on it.

Always set an agenda for your meetings. If your agenda is to ask some questions to determine if the client's needs are a fit for your business, you can use the following statement at a first meeting with a potential client:

"My goal today is to learn a bit more about you, to ask a few questions so I fully understand your project, and to determine if we are a good 'fit' to work together. Does this sound good to you?"

The client will most likely say "yes," unless she has other items to cover, in which case you will add those items to your agenda and make sure you cover them before the meeting is over. Don't worry—I thought this sounded funny to say when I first started doing it, but it really works, and usually my clients respond with

"That sounds great to me!" At worst, a client will likely just add the items she also wants to cover to your agenda.

After getting agreement on the agenda, you can then transition to the business conversation. So how can you shift the discussion without simply bombarding the client with your list of questions?

6. Ask for an update.

Asking for an update is a great way to transition the conversation to business. Ask what, if anything, has changed since you last spoke with the client. You can say something like:

"Is there anything that's changed (with your project) since we last spoke?" (Or "since you last contacted me?")

This is a good way to get an update on the client's situation, to build even more rapport with her, or to offer advice on her situation. The client's answer, if you truly listen, can also help you determine what questions to ask first. Now you can move on to the questions you've already prepared for the client.

7. Question and listen actively.

Now is the phase of the meeting where you can start gathering the information you need to get to know the client, to figure out if the client is a good fit for you, to establish pricing, etc. You can use some of the sample questions I've listed below, but it's important to make a list of questions *before* the meeting to keep yourself on track. You can refer to your list of questions if you find yourself in a situation at the meeting where you're not sure what to ask next. Believe me, if you are nervous at all about the meeting, having a list of questions as a crutch will help you feel comfortable and in control as the meeting progresses.

Below are some specific examples and categories of questions I ask my own clients on a regular basis. You can use these lists and categories of questions to start developing the questions within each category that are most appropriate for your own client calls and meetings.

If you find yourself asking the same questions of each client to develop your pricing or proposals, you can even use the same client worksheet for each call or meeting, and then just "fill in the blanks" for each question/answer as you meet with each client. An example of a client worksheet is shown in my Companion Workbook, which you can download for free as a supplement to this book: https://whattheydontteachyouin-businessschool.lpages.co/freeworkbook/.

In my business, I need specific information before I can come up with a price estimate, or before I can even establish possible package offerings for the client. If a couple wants pricing for a wedding video, I need to ask several questions to determine pricing options for them. As you read my list below, think about why each question is important for developing a proposal for a wedding client. Of course, you'll have different questions for your own product or service, but you can get an idea of how specific you should be, as well as which questions you should ask on every one of your client calls.

General Questions to Determine Pricing:

- What is the wedding date and where is the wedding? Are there multiple locations involved? If so, where are the various locations?
- What time is the ceremony? (Start time and end time)
- What time is the reception? (Start time and end time)
- What time do you want video coverage to start?
- What time do you want video coverage to end?
- What events during the day do you want covered?
- Do you want us to cover just the key events, or also the preparations or events before the ceremony? What about other events during the wedding, such as cocktail hour and general dancing at the reception?

- Do you want partial reception coverage or full reception coverage until the end of the night?

All these logistical items affect the timing of filming for the day, and strongly influence the amount of work we have to do during the editing and production phase, so they are important to establish our pricing. Once I gather this general information, I can then start putting together pricing options based on the amount of time it will take to shoot, edit, and produce the final video. I will typically provide multiple packages for the client to choose from: "good," "better," and "best" package choices, or "least expensive," "more expensive," and "most expensive."

Once I cover the general items, I also ask "emotional" questions to determine the type of person I'm working with, and to help determine where to focus our conversation:

Emotional/Rapport-Building Questions:

- Tell me about your wedding. What do you envision for your day in terms of style? What type of wedding do you want to have? (I.e. elegant, traditional, rustic, etc.)
- Tell me about you and your fiancé. How did you meet? When did you get engaged? How did the proposal happen? Were you surprised? How did you react?

- What parts of the wedding day do you think will be the most important to you? What parts are you most excited about? What video shots are most important to you and your fiancé?

- What will your ceremony be like? What elements do you want to include in the ceremony? (I.e. readings, music, religious aspects, etc.)

- What are your likes/dislikes when it comes to a wedding video? What were your favorite parts (or least favorite parts) of wedding videos you've watched in the past?

- Are any events you're planning for your wedding particularly special to you, or unique to your wedding day?

These types of questions allow me to "get to know" the client and allow me to "steer" the conversation into areas that are most important to her. What is her style? What is most important to her? What does she like most about weddings? These questions are extremely important because I start to learn the true emotions of the person on the other end of the phone. Is she warm and sensitive? Is she traditional? Is she concerned with her guests' impressions of the wedding? How important is her family's opinion to her? How important is her religion? What have her friends done at their weddings that she's liked or disliked?

The answers to these questions will give me a huge amount

of insight into the type of person I'm working with, and will therefore help me know which topics will be important to her in future discussions. The answers will even help me decide which samples of our work to show her, since I'll be able to focus on items she cares about the most. Knowing the answers to these questions will also help me determine if the client is a good fit for my company's offerings, assist in planning for the event, and aid in producing the final video. (I'll make sure to include the items that are most important to her in the final product).

After asking emotional questions, I also ask buying-related questions to determine how the client makes decisions, and to help determine the focus during the later part of our conversation:

Buying/Decision-Making Questions:

- What questions or concerns do you have?
  (It's important to restate, address, and confirm that you've fully addressed each client question or concern *before* moving on to the next question. Do not cut the client off—let her keep talking as long as she needs to get all her questions out before you try to address each question or concern. We'll discuss later in this chapter what to do if the client has no questions.)

- Do you have a budget (specifically for this product or service)? If so, would you like me to try to work within that budget?

  (If the client doesn't have a budget established, that's ok—simply tell her you always like to ask, and then say you'll put together pricing and let her know the options.)

These questions are extremely important to determine how your client is feeling about your product or service.

In some cases, depending on the nature of your business, you may want to add the following question(s) to the above list. The questions below are particularly important when dealing with a corporate client. Note that with a wedding client, one of the first questions I ask is the wedding date; with a corporate client, a definite event date (associated with the production of the video) might not exist:

- What timeframe for delivery/completion are you looking for?
- Is there an event on a specific date by which you need this project done?

These questions are important because you need to know if your client expects the job to be done more quickly than your usual timeframe before you put together your pricing. The answers to these questions give you an opportunity to explain why your typical timeframe may be longer than what the client is asking for, and then you can reach an agreeable timeframe with your client. Or, if you want to try to meet the client's expedited timeframe, you can consider charging an extra fee for quicker delivery.

Again, as you are going through the meeting, don't just run down a list of questions. It is very important to respond to what the customer is saying, to show the client that you're actively listening by responding to her (*uh huh*, *right*, and *sure* are good, quick words to show her you're listening without interrupting). You can also show you're listening by taking notes and offering your reaction, where appropriate, to certain comments the client makes. We'll cover even more on the questioning and listening topic in Chapter 5.

7a. Ask follow-up questions.

After you've gone through your questions and taken notes, ask follow-up questions as necessary. If you don't understand something the client has told you, ask the same question again in a different way to make sure you know what she's saying. I know we all have the temptation to avoid follow-up questions because we don't want to "look stupid," but people really do appreciate you trying to understand their situation clearly. Using phrases like these can help in a situation where you need more clarity on a client's answer:

- "I want to make sure I'm clear on . . . "
- "Let me make sure I understand what you said about . . . "
- "I'm not sure if I fully understood what you said about _____. Can you explain that again, please?"

8. Ask if the client has questions.

You should also ask the client if she has any questions when you've finished with yours, or whenever you're not sure what to ask next. This tactic is designed to gauge the client's interest level in the conversation and to see what she is most interested in. It is also a good segue into describing your products/services, explaining how the process of working with you typically goes, and reviewing what your final product/deliverable includes. I usually say something like this:

"I know I've been asking a lot of questions, and you've given me lots of great information. Let me stop for a moment—are there any questions you'd like to ask me at this point?"

If the client has no questions, go to Step 8a.

If the client *does* have questions, go to Step 8b.

8a. Client has no questions:

If the client says she has no questions, describe your top three frequently asked questions (FAQs) or your process in terms the client will understand, accentuating the differentiators of your company and the benefits the client will receive.

I usually say something like:

"Since you have no questions just yet, how about if I go over the top three frequently-asked questions our clients usually ask us?"

FAQs and Differentiators

During this process, make sure to explain things the average person may not know about your business that is distinct from others—what we call "differentiators." Also, and even more importantly, explain to the client *why* those items are of benefit. Again, it's about the client; it's not about you. Here are a few examples of frequently asked questions and differentiators I often cover with my clients:

1. "Who will be shooting my wedding?" or "Do you subcontract to other shooters?"

My answer: "We never subcontract our filming or editing to anyone else. That can cause numerous problems, but unfortunatcly many other companics do 'sub out.' Your wedding day is simply too important to risk not capturing properly, and since those once-in-a-lifetime memories can never be recaptured again, we don't trust anyone else to capture it the way we do. My business partner and I filmed and edited all the samples of work that you see online and on our website. No matter who you talk to about video, you should always ask to see samples of the *specific* person's work who is filming and editing, so you know what you'll be getting in the final product."

I specifically mention this point as a key differentiator because I know that many of our competitors do subcontract the shooting, and we are at an advantage because we do not. I also explain why this is important to the customer (so they don't miss any of these special, once-in-a-lifetime moments).

2. "How many cameras do you use, and why?"

My answer: "We always use multiple cameras at every event. This ensures that in the final video, you're not looking at a single shot of the back of your heads during the entire ceremony. Instead, you receive a final product that shows different angles, includes both close-up and wider shots, and it's like watching a real movie—*your* movie! It's so much more fun for you to watch! The use of multiple cameras also ensures that you don't miss anything important. When your favorite relative decides to step into the aisle in front of one of our cameras during the ceremony to snap a photo of your first kiss, you still won't miss those kinds of key moments in your video because we have another camera angle to cut to during the editing process. Believe me, this happens (it is a live event after all!), so multiple cameras are an insurance policy for *you*."

I specifically mention this point as a key differentiator because I know that many of our competitors use a single camera, and the final product is sub-par because of that. Again, I accentuate what we do differently from the competition and why this is important for the customer, using examples that someone outside my business can understand.

3. "What is included in the final product?"

My answer: "As for the final deliverable, we provide both a highlights film *and* a full-length, professionally edited documentary video, which includes the key events of your day and much more. Many companies provide *only* a highlights film, but we provide the 'best of both worlds' for our clients. That way, you can watch not just highlights of your day, but also your first dance again, all the toasts and speeches, and your full ceremony whenever you want to! It is a lot more work to produce a video like this, but our clients find that it's well worth it to have all these moments on video because they miss so much throughout the day."

I specifically mention this point as a key differentiator because I know that my competition typically provides much less than we do as a final product (typically only a short highlights film *or* a highlights film with raw, unedited footage). I also explain why this is important to the client (so they can see the full moments as well as a highlights recap from the day).

An alternative to the above method of reviewing your FAQs is to ask the client a slightly different question to achieve the same result:

"Would it be helpful if I walk you through the process of what we do, how we do it, and what you'll receive for a final product?"

With this method, you can walk the client through your typical process, as well as explain what your final deliverable typically includes, while weaving your frequently asked questions or differentiators into your explanation. Of course, my explanation of the process to the client is going to include my top three differentiators I reviewed above—the fact that we use multiple cameras, that we do all the work ourselves (vs. sub-contracting), and that the final product includes *both* a highlights film *and* a professionally edited documentary video. With this alternative method, I achieve the same result as the first method in a slightly different way. Use the method that is most comfortable for you.

Finally, ask the client (again!) if she has any questions. After reviewing our top three FAQs or walking her through the process of working with us and describing what we typically do (always focusing on what we do that our competition doesn't do), I then ask if she has any questions. Yes, I ask again! You can say something like:

"Now that I've walked you through our process and given you an idea of what our final product looks like, does this generate any additional questions you'd like to ask?" or "Now that I've gone through some of the questions we're asked most frequently, does this generate any additional questions you'd like to ask?"

If yes, go through the process described in Step 8b until you address all client questions (list, address, and get agreement that you've answered each question satisfactorily). If no, move on to Step 9.

8b. Client has questions:

- Make a list of all questions or concerns the client has before addressing each one.
- Address each question or concern separately.
- Confirm and get agreement that you've addressed each question or concern before moving forward with the conversation.

Remember, questions from the client are good. Questions mean that your client is interested in possibly buying from you.

A great way to respond to questions is by saying,

- "That's actually a great question."
- "Thanks for asking that question."
- "I wish more people would ask that question, because it's very important."

If you're not sure exactly what the client is asking, you can re-phrase the question back to her to make sure you understand it. Here are a few ways to re-phrase a question:

- "So what I think you're asking is . . ."
- "So what you're concerned about is _____. Is that correct?"
- "Let me make sure I understand your question . . ."

Let your client express all her questions or concerns before you try to address them. It's difficult, but instead of trying to answer her first question immediately, ask her if she has any additional questions. Write them all down, and when the client's list is finished, *then* you can address each question or concern.

Once you've addressed each concern, confirm that the client is satisfied with how you have answered each one. You can get confirmation by asking:

- "Does that help address your concern about x, y, or z?"
- "Did I address the concerns you expressed, or do you have additional questions for me about x, y, or z?"

Finally, ask the client (again!) if she has any questions. After listing out each question or concern, addressing each question/ concern, and confirming that you've addressed each of the client's questions satisfactorily, I then ask if she has any other questions. Yes, I ask her again! You can say something like: "Now that we've gone through your list of questions, did I answer everything, or do you have any additional questions?"

If yes, repeat the process described in Step 8b above (list, address, and get agreement that you've answered each question satisfactorily). If no, move on to Step 9.

Be patient with your client; she may never have purchased a service like yours in the past. Questions are good—not only do they mean your client is interested, but they also give you an opportunity to earn more trust and to start setting expectations with your client!

9. Offer assistance and referrals.

Once you've answered your client's questions and concerns, but before you wrap up the meeting or call, always offer to help the client in any other way you can. Offer her assistance or recommendations if it's applicable to her situation or project. For example, if I'm talking with a bride, I'll ask the following question, since she may never have gone through the process of planning a wedding before:

"Are there any other items you need for your wedding that I

could help you with? I know plenty of people in the industry who I trust that I'd be happy to refer you to if there's anything else you need—calligraphers, florists, musicians, photographers, etc."

After our meeting, I then send a follow-up email with the referrals the client requests. Your clients will appreciate your willingness to help them, and your ability to give them trusted referrals—as you would with a friend—always makes it about *them*, not about you.

10. Establish the next steps.

At the end of every meeting or call, always establish the next steps for all parties, along with projected timeframes for those steps. In other words, once the meeting is over, what will happen next? Will you follow up with pricing options, or will you send the client additional info that she's requested, such as samples of your work, or will you write a proposal or contract and send it to her for review? You can say something like this to broach the subject of next steps:

"I think we've covered everything we need to cover today. So what do you think is the most appropriate next step for us at this point?"

Often when I ask the above question of my clients, they ask me for a proposal and/or they give me "buying signals," such as asking what types of payment we accept or what type of deposit we require. When the client asks you about payment and deposits, that's a great sign that they are interested in buying from you!

If you need to send the client more information as a follow-up, give her an estimated timeframe in which she'll receive these items from you. Again, ask for her agreement on timeframe by saying something like:

"I should have the proposal completed by the end of the week. Does that work for you?"

Does the client still owe you additional info before you can finish a proposal or pricing? If so, outline her next steps and get agreement on a timeframe in which she can complete those action items.

—

We've covered a ton of information in this chapter: the importance of determining a goal for your meeting, preparing for the call or meeting, questions to ask, and the steps to go through during the client meeting.

In addition to the client worksheet in my Companion Workbook—which will help you outline what to ask your client and determine the information you need before your client meeting—you'll also find a reference chart outlining each of the steps we've covered in this chapter (see "How to Handle the First Client Meeting in 10 Easy Steps").

Now it's time to put together a proposal, a contract, or written pricing. What kinds of items do you need to put in writing? Why is it important to have it all in writing, anyway? What do you need to discuss with the client *before* putting the proposal or contract together? We'll discuss these extremely important topics in Chapter 4.

But before you move on, ask yourself the following:

What are the top five questions you are going to write down and plan to ask your potential client in advance of the first meeting with her?

CHAPTER 4

PUT IT IN WRITING

"Until the contract is signed, nothing is real."
—Glenn Danzig, musician

"A verbal contract isn't worth the paper it's written on."
—Samuel Goldwyn, film producer

You may not want to hear this, but an essential part of good customer service is putting agreements in writing. A written agreement protects you and documents terms and conditions in the event of a problem, but that's not all it does. Just the process of working together on the details of an agreement is essential for a good client relationship, because it ensures that you and your client are both on the same page. You've set expectations along the way, and now you need to put it all in writing—that's the only way to avoid misunderstandings during the course of your relationship or project. Solidifying your discussions with documentation is a key part of the process of setting expectations.

If you're not a lawyer, you probably have lots of questions about a contract or written agreement:

- What do you need to discuss with the client before writing it?
- Why is it important to talk about these items with the client beforehand?
- What specific items need to go into the agreement?

I'll address these questions in this chapter.

One important note before I start: you don't need a lawyer to write a contract. Write out the terms in your own words, numbering each topic. If you want to look at a sample contract, plenty of websites offer examples so you can easily draft one yourself. The important thing is to clearly and simply phrase the elements of the agreement, make sure the client has read it, and get your signature and his, plus the date. Now you have an enforceable contract!

1. Discuss issues *before* you draft the contract.

Make sure you discuss these items with the client, and then get them in writing:

- What is the "scope of work," what services will you provide, and what specific deliverables will you give the client?
- What are the payment terms and when are payments due? What forms of payment do you accept?
- What is your schedule for completing the project? Do you have a firm deadline, or have you agreed on a range of time in which you estimate or guarantee completion?
- Are there items the client needs to provide? By what date do you need to receive them? If you do not receive the required items by the due date, how will that affect the expected timeframe for completion, the project process or flow, etc.?
- What general or legal disclaimers and provisions should you include?

If you don't think about these items beforehand, and document them later, you are setting yourself up for trouble. Believe me, you don't want to be in a situation where the client says, "But you told me x, y, or z regarding the pricing . . ." and then you have no documentation of the original price quote or your actual discussion with the client.

You likely have already discussed big issues such as pricing with the client, but maybe you haven't discussed all the "what ifs":

- What happens if the client tries to cancel the contract? In what cases is cancellation allowed? In what timeframe? Will the client get any money back or a refund in the case of cancellation? What is reasonable (or what is the industry standard) in terms of refunds?
- What happens if you cannot show up at the client's event or you cannot complete the project due to illness, injury, or an unforeseen act of God? What recourse does the client have? What will you do to rectify that situation or to find a substitute vendor for the event?
- What extra fees are there, and under what circumstances do those additional fees kick in? What inclusions or exclusions are there within your overall fee structure?

You need to consider all these contingencies *before* you start the project. An essential element of good customer service is being clear and upfront—never surprise a client!

For example, what if you typically estimate four to six weeks for completion, but you never told the client that? Then he contacts you two weeks later to see if the project is done. Do you really want to have that discussion with the client at that time? You need to agree to a timeframe, verbally and in writing, *before* you get started—and you want to have provisions around that timeframe so the client understands when and how that timeframe might be affected. Get that in writing before he says, "But I thought it would only take two weeks!"

2. Keep a paper trail.

Before you draft the contract, make sure you keep a "paper trail" of any discussions. Keep all your emails to and from the client in a separate folder for each project. Document your conversations with the client in an email to yourself; the time stamp will be helpful in determining what you agreed to and when.

3. Draft a thorough contract.

In general, your contracts, agreements, or documentation should cover the following elements:

- Services/products/scope of work
- Specific deliverables to the client
- Pricing/fees and payment terms (including cancellation policy and terms)
- Timeframe for completion

- Items the client needs to provide and when, what will happen if he doesn't provide them by the due date, and how that affects the timeframe or project flow
- Expenses/accommodations (note who is responsible for these)
- Other terms and conditions (provisions and disclaimers)
- Notice/signature/date (including contact info for both parties)

You should have already discussed most of these items with your client; the contract-writing process merely forces you to specify them clearly in writing. And, conversely, having a standard contract form will remind you to discuss those items with the client and get agreement on them ahead of time, before moving forward with the project.

When I first started my business, there were times I sat down to draft a proposal or a contract, only to realize that I needed additional information from the client before I could write it. This meant I had forgotten to ask some questions in the client meeting. The process of writing contracts, once you do it a few times, will help you remember items you need to ask the client in the meeting. Over time, you'll start to see the lines of the contract in your head as you're speaking with the client, and you'll begin to ask the key questions to fill in the blanks. If you're afraid you'll forget to ask about certain items, bring a blank copy of your contract with you to the call or meeting, keep it in a private folder, and refer to it if necessary as you go through the meeting with the client.

4. Explain the importance of a contract to the client.

What if the client doesn't want to sign a contract? You might be tempted to skip it if you need the business, but a written agreement needs to be a condition of doing business together. First, try using the term "agreement" instead of "contract" when speaking with your client. For some reason, the word "agreement" seems less intimidating than the word "contract" to most people, so using the former will help soften the tone of the discussion.

Explain that the agreement's purpose is to make sure the expectations are clear on *both* sides, and to ensure that you understand everything about the project correctly. Assure the client that he will have the opportunity to ask questions or request changes to the agreement before proceeding. This doesn't mean you have to make all the changes the client asks for, but going through this process and addressing his contractual concerns will give you a clear idea of how reasonable (or unreasonable) he actually is, and then you can decide whether you really want to enter into this business relationship. If you've done your job of setting expectations and you're dealing with a reasonable person, most of your clients will have no concerns, or minimal concerns, and they will simply send you back the signed contract.

The process of addressing the client's concerns about the contract will bring potential issues to light, once again, *before* the start of the project. You should welcome the opportunity to answer the client's questions! I know it's often unpleasant to have these discussions with the client, but it's so much better to get them out of the way beforehand—compared to having a dissatisfied customer who disputes the amount of his final bill or who tries to cancel mid-project. Addressing the client's concerns about the contract will also help you consider issues you hadn't thought of before, and you can decide how you should handle them—before you're in the middle of the project.

Here's an example. I recently had a client bring up a very important issue that I hadn't been including in my contracts in the past: what happens if you can't shoot my event due to illness or some unforeseen circumstance? Will you find us someone of equal caliber to replace you? Will you give us a refund? What if we don't agree to the substitute offer? Even though I've never had to cancel a contracted event (knock on wood!), his questions forced me to consider what I would do in that scenario, and to consider what a reasonable solution would be. The client and I mutually agreed on some reasonable language to add into the agreement (language that worked for both parties), and both of us moved forward with a level of comfort about the arrangement.

The process of reviewing the contract with the client also brings to light negative issues that you may not have seen before with a particular client. What do you do if you see how unreasonable or inflexible a client can be? Isn't it better to know this about the client beforehand, so you can decide if you even want to do business with that type of person?

Here's another example: I once had a potential client who seemed extremely picky in our initial meetings about what she wanted, and was rather negative. Every time I walked away from a conversation with her, I just didn't feel good. I started to feel extremely stressed every time I got off the phone with her— and this was before the project even started! I contemplated whether or not I wanted to do business with this person, and whether it would even be worth any amount of money she paid. I continued the discussions with her, but when it came to the contractual discussions, I fully realized that my concerns were valid, and I knew that I truly did *not* want to do business with her.

It turned out this client wanted certain items for free that she had never mentioned before (items that I could *not* provide for free). She also wanted a clause in the contract stating that if she were dissatisfied with the final product *for any reason*, we would give her *all* her money back (of course, after all the work had already been done and all our costs were already incurred). Sounds like a reasonable client, right? Hardly! She truly seemed to be looking for what could go wrong with our relationship and what her legal recourses would be, instead of reacting the way most clients do when they sign with us: positive about what will go right and excited to see what we're going to produce for them.

As difficult as it was, I forced myself to explain to this client that I sensed her lack of trust in us—despite all our phone calls and meetings, and despite viewing many samples of our work and multiple client testimonials. I explained that I just didn't think it was a good "fit" for us to work together. As hard as it was to refuse a client and to walk away from the deal, I broke off the relationship and felt a huge sense of relief after doing so. It just wasn't worth it. If I hadn't had the conversation about contractual issues with this client, these issues might never have been solidified in my brain enough to cut things off before it was too late. Don't ignore your "inner voice" that nags you when something doesn't feel right.

—

In this chapter, we've covered a lot of information about contracts. Now that you have a handle on why you need to "put it in writing," what to include in the contract, and what to discuss with your client before signing, we're going to take a step back in the next chapter.

Why? Well, some of you may need to meet with your client more than once before getting him to sign the contract or before he agrees to work with you. Maybe you're finding that the next step after the first meeting with the client does not always result in a request for a contract, but the first meeting results in a second meeting. What do you do in that case? Perhaps you need to delve further into questioning and listening techniques because you're not at the contract phase yet.

In these kinds of cases, you need to discover the client's concerns or "pain points." You'll also need to actively respond to the client based on his behavior, and determine what to do when he only asks about pricc, or when he gives you absolutely no idea if he wants to work with you by the end of the meeting. I'll cover these sensitive topics in Chapter 5.

Ask yourself the following question before moving on to the next chapter:

What are the top three items you are going to start putting in writing with your clients?

CHAPTER 5

QUESTIONING AND LISTENING

"Successful people ask better questions, and as a result, they get better answers."

—Anthony Robbins, motivational speaker

"If you want to be listened to, you should put in time listening."

—Marge Piercy, poet and social activist

In Chapter 3, we talked about various questions you can ask in your first meeting with the client: general, emotional/rapport-building, and buying/decision-making questions. We also discussed the importance of listening.

In this chapter, we'll go into more detail on the questioning and listening topic, so you know the types of questions that will provide a clearer indication of where you stand with your client before you walk away from the meeting. We'll review the following:

- How to identify the client's "pain points"—problems you can solve—and how to determine the client's key decision-making criteria for your product or service.
- How to listen and respond appropriately to the client, and how to "mirror" her behavior, pace, and tone of voice as needed.
- What to do if the client has no questions, or if the only question is "how much does it cost?"

You've already asked your client some questions, and you have the key information you need to price out the project. But what questions can you ask that will tell you even more about her decision-making process? What questions will elicit clues that the client is actually going to buy from you, versus your competitor? When I haven't asked questions to determine a potential client's "pain points," I've often walked away wondering if I'm going to get her business. But when I *have* asked these questions, I've had a much clearer picture of whether or not the client is highly interested in my services before the meeting ends.

1. Ask "pain point" questions.

- "Why is [your product or service] important to you?"
- "What is most important about [your product or service] to you, your spouse, your parents, or your colleagues?" (Ask this question to every person involved in the decision-making, as each person may have a different answer.)
- "What experiences have you had in the past with [your product or service]?"

Don't assume you know the answers to these questions. When I've asked—and simply waited for each person in the meeting to respond—the answers have revealed the most telling information about my clients.

Think about it. The client's answers to "Why is a wedding video important to you?" or "What experiences have you had in the past with videography services?" could reveal that the client's grandparents cannot attend the wedding because they are ill, which might be why the client wants a wedding video in the first place. It could reveal that the bride's sister hired an amateur videographer who never delivered her wedding video, and therefore the client now realizes how important it is to hire a professional videographer. It could reveal that the client wants to preserve these precious memories for future generations, because her father has already passed away and she has no video footage of him when he was alive. Or it could tell me that the bride wants to see the groom's face on video to get a glimpse of how he reacts when she walks down the aisle (something she won't see when it's actually taking place).

Knowing why video is important and what the client's past experience is with your product or service provides key information, and the client's responses can lead you into your next questions, as well as reveal the "pain point" of the client.

A "pain point" is a problem your client has that your business can solve. What "pain" does the client feel that will induce her to hire you or buy from you? If you can hone in on the "pain" or concerns your client is feeling, and focus on that problem as you're explaining your services, you are more likely to get the client's business due to the emotional connection you've established and the solution you provide for her problem.

For example, if the bride's "pain" is that she is afraid she is going to miss certain key emotional moments during the day (such as the groom's reaction before she walks down the aisle), then I will carefully select and send her video samples with images of grooms' emotional reactions. If her pain point is that she lost her father and she wants to preserve memories for future generations, I will show her emotional family moments, such as a special dance honoring grandparents or family elders, a poignant dance between a father and daughter, or a heartfelt toast that mentions a relative who has passed away. I will carefully select the best and most tender samples that will emotionally affect the bride when she watches them, based on the "pain points" she has expressed during our discussions.

Here's another example from my business, one that every parent of a child who participates in dance, theater, or the performing arts can relate to:

A new dance studio owner ("Jen") called me this past spring to inquire about our professional videography services for her upcoming dance recital. One of my most important questions for Jen during our first phone call was, "What experience have you had in the past with video services for your recitals?" Jen's answer was typical of what I hear from many of our dance studio clients. She responded, "I can't see the dancers' faces in the video because they're 'whited out' on stage. The overall quality wasn't very good—the videographer only used one camera, the video quality was poor, and he missed or cut off key moments or key choreography that happened on stage."

These are "pain points" and problems I hear about on a regular basis from dance studio clients who need my services. Knowing these key items up front allows me to focus on the solution my company provides to these problems, and what we do to avoid these kinds of mistakes, when I explain my services to the client. In this case, I proceeded to explain to Jen our use of multiple, high-definition cameras (and how that achieves better video quality); our use of manual settings on our cameras (and how that avoids "white out"); and our use of a meticulous editing process, during which we carefully select the most appropriate shots from each camera used at a recital (and how that prevents missing key choreography). Jen is now a repeat client who, after seeing the extremely high-quality video we produced for her the first year, quickly booked us for her recital again the following year.

Whether you own a bakery, or work as a professional photographer, or run an event venue, you can use this tactic by showing samples of your cakes, your photos, or areas of your property that your client is most interested in and target her "pain point." Your client will then feel an emotional connection to your product or service and you'll be solving her problems—as a result, she'll be more inclined to use your service over your competition. Once again, it's all about the client. Adjust your plans on which samples of your work to show once you hear what is most important to her. You may not have planned your presentation this way, but if you listen to the client and adjust according to what she is telling you, you will be more likely to get her business.

After asking "pain point" questions, ask the following key question:

"What will be the key factors or most important criteria in your decision-making process?"

The answer to this question will tell you a lot, so once you ask it, force yourself to be quiet and let your client answer the question. She may say that the relationship with the company she hires is the most important factor, or perhaps it's the quality of work, or the company's reputation in the industry, or the dreaded "best price." Wouldn't it be extremely helpful to know where you stand with the client before the meeting ends?

Ask this question at the *end* of the meeting, after you've had a chance to build the relationship and have earned the client's trust. If you've done your job during the meeting—getting at the client's "pain" and gearing your presentation towards that—she is very unlikely to say "the best price" is the most important factor. However, if she does lead with price as the top decision-making factor, and your company is not the cheapest option, this gives you a chance to explain *why* your company is more expensive than others—before the client makes her final decision.

In my case, I am definitely not the least expensive vendor in my industry, so "the best price" answer can feel like a deal-breaker. However, if I've built the client relationship by asking the right questions and adjusting appropriately to her responses, the client usually doesn't balk when she finds out we're not the cheapest option.

Once you've achieved a connection and built the relationship, your client may instead say something like this: "Well, price is important, but I don't want to sacrifice a good relationship with the company just for the sake of a low price." Yes! That's the answer you want to hear! Or she might say, "Well, price is kind of important, but the quality of the work has to be there first before we even consider the price." Again, yes! These types of responses mean the client values the quality of your work and/or the emotional connection the two of you have built during the meeting.

If I've gone through the entire process we've discussed in this book with the client and her answer is still "the lowest price is most important," then I know this is definitely not my ideal client. My company provides extremely high-quality services, and we do much more than the average company, which means our products take longer to produce. Clients who truly care about quality continue to hire us. People or companies who only care about price (and not quality) do not hire us, and that's okay. As hard as it is, remember that not everyone will be your client. You cannot be all things to all people, so figure out your niche in the market where you surpass the competition and try to excel there.

2. Actively listen and respond.

So how do you actively listen and respond to what your client is really saying?

First, don't just run down a list of questions—have a *conversation* with the client. If she answers a certain question in a way that leads you to another topic, go with it and adjust your line of questioning to ask the next most logical question. Use your original question list as a guide, so when you need another question to ask, you can choose one from the list. Again, it's about the client, not about you, so adjust by letting her talk about topics that she finds interesting, and ask follow-up questions about those topics, before moving on to your next question. If you are really listening, you may even notice that the client will answer some of the questions you originally had on your list, without you even asking!

Another way to respond to your client is to "mirror" the pace and tone of your client's voice, if you can do that fairly easily. Years ago, before I started my own business, a trainee in the company I was working for shadowed me for the day and attended client meetings with me. After one of our client meetings, the trainee said to me, "I noticed in the meeting that your voice was so much softer than the way you usually talk . . . why?" I asked her if she noticed that the client was much more soft-spoken than I am. When she said yes, I explained to her that I decreased the level of my voice to make the client more comfortable and to "mirror" the way she talks. I further explained that if I had talked in my typical louder voice, it would have been too overwhelming for this particular client, so I purposely "turned it down a notch."

You can also try this technique with your speaking pace. Have you ever been in a meeting with someone who talks so fast that you just want her to slow down and explain everything to you slowly and clearly? Or, in the opposite case, with someone who takes so long explaining and re-explaining that you're looking at your watch because you want her to get to the point? Try to speed up or slow down as needed and keep pace with her. If you handle things at a pace she is used to or most comfortable with, she will in turn be more comfortable with you.

Finally, be on alert for non-verbal signals from the client. In other words, does she look bored? Is she looking at her watch or constantly checking her phone? Is her body language giving you cues that she is not interested or not listening? If you see these types of signals, adjust accordingly and try to re-engage the client in the discussion.

3. Address the price question.

If the client has no questions for you—or if her only question is the price—what do you do? You can say something like:

"I'll be sure to get to the pricing in a moment, but before we do that, do you have any other questions about our product or service, the process of working with us, or the final deliverable?"

If she has additional questions, answer those questions before moving forward, weaving your differentiators or FAQs into your responses, as we discussed in Chapter 3.

Always try to think about the top three things most people ask about your business *or* develop a list of three things you definitely want your client to know about before making a decision. What do you do differently from your competition? How does the final product differ? Why are these differentiators important to your customer?

Maybe your final product offers something unique that others in your industry don't offer—focus on that. Maybe you use local or organic ingredients that no one else in your industry is using—focus on that. Maybe your company has a special certification or is trained in a skill that no other companies in your industry are—focus on that. Maybe you have won industry awards or you have relevant background experience that others in your industry do not—focus on that. Once you decide on your three topics, you must always remember to explain *why* these points are beneficial to your client. Explain each item quickly and succinctly, to ensure that your client doesn't feel that you are simply trying to avoid the price question.

If the client has no additional questions about your product or service and her only remaining question is the price, you can address any remaining questions you might have before quoting a price by saying something like this:

"I'll need just a few more details before I can give you an exact price . . . can I ask you a few final questions so I can determine pricing options for you?"

Then ask your client the remaining questions that will help you develop your pricing.

It is important to understand that your clients may only be asking you about price because they truly do not know what else to ask. They may have never purchased your type of service or product before. When you haven't purchased something before (and perhaps you haven't done any research on the product or service yet), what do you ask? You ask about price because you have no idea what else to inquire about. Once you've done your research or talked to a few people about the product or service, you develop more questions, but until that point, you just ask, "How much does it cost?" Try to not be offended by this question, and try to give the client the benefit of the doubt by remembering that she may simply not know what else to ask you. Clients will understand when you explain that you need some details about the project and what they're looking for before you can give them an exact price.

If you need more information before establishing the price, you'll need to get those details before quoting an exact price to your client. You can offer a price "estimate" as a start, but that can be risky because the client will typically remember the first number you gave her.

If you can't give the client an exact price for the whole project yet, but you want to provide some sort of pricing information, you can at least tell her your regular rates that aren't likely to change—hourly rates, rental rates for your space, deposits required, average expenditure per client, starting prices, most popular current package price, etc. It's important to charge what you said you would charge, so you're better off making sure you have quoted the right price, or as close to the right price as possible, the first time. It's also critical that you're able to clearly explain and justify your pricing with your client. Why?

If a client receives your invoice with a charge she expected, she'll likely pay the invoice immediately. If, on the other hand, she sees a completely different figure on the invoice—and you never explained the amount to her—you might not get paid quickly, paid the full amount, or paid at all. One thing is sure: you'll have an unhappy client who won't refer you to others. If you frequently have clients complaining about the cost once you've finished the project, that's a sign that you need to consider your pricing structure from a new angle, revisit the way you are communicating your pricing to clients, or rework the way your contract is written.

Keep in mind that your pricing structure and your contracts will be a "work in progress." With each new project, you'll start to learn what you forgot to charge, what you didn't tell the client ahead of time, and other issues that you failed to discuss with your client. (Also, your rates may decrease if you're not getting enough work, or increase as you gain more experience or your services become more in demand.) How you learn from the mistakes you make, and use them to improve your communication of pricing with your clients in the future, is what matters the most.

Once you've asked enough questions to gather the necessary details to price out each project, determined your client's "pain points," learned her key decision-making criteria, and shared your company's differentiators, you'll be well-equipped to more confidently discuss your pricing both verbally and in writing.

—

In this chapter, we've gone into more detail on the questioning and listening topic, so you'll have a clearer indication of where you stand with your client before you walk away from the meeting. We also covered getting at your client's pain points, how to "mirror" your client's pace and tone as needed, and what to do when the client's only question is about price. So now that you've had your meeting with the client, you've given her pricing, and you've signed a contract that both of you are happy with, you're ready to start the project!

In Chapter 6, we'll review the importance of follow-up communication and updating your client throughout the course of the project, meeting your projected timelines, and responding to and dealing with issues that may arise during the job.

What are three questions you can ask at the client meeting to discover your client's "pain"?

CHAPTER 6

FOLLOW-UP COMMUNICATION AND CLIENT UPDATES

"Diligent follow-up and follow-through will set you apart from the crowd and communicate excellence."
—John C. Maxwell, author and pastor

Have you ever bought something, or sent in a payment for a product or service you've agreed to buy, and then worried whether you'd made the right decision? Or have you ever worked with an extremely communicative business that goes silent after receiving your money? We've all felt buyer's remorse at one time or another. After I receive a client's payment, I remind myself of that terrible feeling and always strive to make my clients feel good about their purchases. Make an effort to provide just as much communication with your client after receiving the first payment as you did before the client signed the contract. Update the client on a regular basis. In turn, the client's comfort level with you and your company will increase.

Perhaps you think there's nothing much to tell the client until the job really gets going. Believe me, there is *always* something you can tell the client.

In this chapter, we'll talk about how and when to update your client, and on what kinds of items—even when it seems like you have nothing to say.

1. How and why should I update the client?

For starters, email your clients to thank them for sending in their first payment or signed contract. Tell them you wanted to confirm receipt of the payment, or paperwork, and emphasize how excited you are to work with them! Let them know they're all set for the moment, and tell them when they can expect to hear from you again. It's a simple gesture, but contacting clients to let them know their payment or contract arrived safely and that you're looking forward to working with them goes a long way.

In my own emails, I thank my clients and tell them I'll be getting back in touch within a range of time to confirm certain details prior to their event. I also remind them to get back to me with items I'll need before starting their project. This sets expectations, instead of leaving clients hanging about what to do next, or wondering when they should expect to hear from me again. The mantra I recommend living by is:

Get to them *before* they get to you.

You definitely don't want the client emailing or texting you to ask, "Did you receive my check?" or "Did you get the contract I sent?" or "I haven't heard from you in a while . . . what's happening?" Validate the client's positive feelings about your company well *before* he feels the need to check in with you. It only takes a few minutes to contact the client to say that a payment arrived, and to establish what the next step will be. If you follow up quickly, he will immediately feel good about the decision to use your company.

If for some reason your client does happen to get to you before you get to him somewhere along the project timeline (it will happen—no one is perfect!), make sure to respond to him with the same urgency you had before he hired you. Don't leave the client hanging, especially if it sounds like he has an issue to discuss. Even if you don't have a complete answer for the client right away, you can respond with something like:

"Thanks so much for your message. I'm out of the office this afternoon at a client meeting, but I wanted to get back to you as soon as possible about this. I promise to call you as soon as I return to the office later tonight after 5:00 pm. Just let me know if there is a better time to reach you by phone this evening."

If the client has a truly urgent question, of course you can't use this response, but you'll need to judge the urgency of the issue. If the issue truly is urgent, call the client on the next break during your meeting, or as soon as the meeting is over. Even if the client thinks it's urgent, the issue may not be absolutely time-sensitive, but you still need to reply with a response in a reasonable period of time. How quickly do you normally respond to client emails or voicemails? Try to generally stick with your typical response time in these cases as well, so as not to leave the client hanging.

Remember, your client doesn't necessarily know your process of completing jobs, so you need to help him with that. He may think his questions are urgent, but you may have five other client jobs to complete before his. This client is not your only one (even though he may think he is!), but you still need to respond quickly to let him know when you'll be getting back to him. At least he will know you got his message while he is waiting for you to reply! That initial response should hold him off for a while, which is what you want to achieve. You don't want the client getting increasingly worried because he hasn't heard from you, and a simple reply lets him know you haven't forgotten about the message.

2. How often should I update the client?

Once the project starts, continue to update your client regularly. Set a regular timeframe—maybe once a week, or every few days. The important thing is to "get to them *before* they get to you." If you're unsure about how often to send your client updates, ask your client if weekly updates (or another time schedule that you think will work well for the project) works for them. Don't leave the client wondering what's going on with the project. In each communication with him, always set an expectation or a next step so he knows either what is coming next or when he can expect to hear from you again. This will prevent getting those dreaded emails from your clients demanding an immediate update on their projects.

3. What kinds of items can I use to update the client?

Here are some examples of items you can communicate to your clients in your updates:

- Confirm receipt of a payment or a signed contract
- Outline next steps for the project or action items from a client meeting
- Provide a status update on the project
- Send an estimated project timeline or communicate changes to a timeline
- Ask for an item you need from the client to complete the project
- Tell the client how much you love how the final product is turning out (even if it's not done yet!)
- Confirm important details prior to a client event
- Ask questions that come up during the project
- Provide an expected completion timeframe or shipment timeframe
- Confirm that you've shipped an item to the client and provide a tracking number

Here's a great example of what *not* to do as it relates to updating clients:

I'll never forget my last experience buying car tires at a not-so-small business that will remain unnamed. The less-than-cheerful salesman processing orders at the counter told my husband and me that it would take about an hour for our new tires to be installed. The good news is that he also told us we could go shopping in the store adjacent to the tire center while we waited, and he gave us a ticket to scan at any barcode reader in the store to check the status of our job. Sounds good, right?

The bad news is that we checked the status of our job several times after we finished shopping, and the job continued to be "in progress." Although we headed back to the waiting area in the tire shop and the initial hour had well passed, no one updated us on the job or gave us a clue as to why it was taking so long. It would have been a simple but thoughtful gesture to come over to us and say, "I know you've been waiting a while—let me check on your job for you. I'll be right back." Or he could have said, "It shouldn't be too much longer on your job—sorry we're running a bit over the estimated time, but it shouldn't take more than another 15 minutes." Any personal attention at all would have made the situation so much better.

Of course, you need to be smart about what you say when updating the customer. You should only provide information you know is true—don't say it will only be another 15 minutes if you know it will take another hour. In that case, you need to address the issue and explain to the customer why it will take a whole additional hour than initially estimated.

Don't avoid the issue and don't make excuses—be honest. If you're the tire salesman and there's a problem with the car, address it now. In this case, there was a problem with one of the tire valves that was holding up the job, but the salesman did not bring that problem to our attention until much later, when we were already boiling with frustration because we had no idea why the job was taking more than twice as long as estimated! The story got worse from there, but I'll skip the details. Bottom line: if you say you're going to do something in an hour, or in a week, or by next Monday, DO IT in that timeframe! If you can't achieve the initial deadline, you need to explain why to the customer!

This story brings me to another of my mantras:

Do what you say you're going to do, when you say you're going to do it!

If for some unforeseen reason you can't complete the task on time, you need to get back in touch with the client *before* the initial deadline, explain why the job can't be completed in the initial timeframe, apologize (always!), and tell the client when the task will actually be done. Be careful about what you tell him—you don't want to put yourself in a situation where you miss a deadline twice. That would certainly result in a frustrated, upset client. Be realistic about estimating your timeframes, and typically the client will understand.

If you can, add just a little bit of time to the estimated timeframe. If you think the job will realistically take a maximum of 10 more minutes, tell the client it will take about 15 to 20 minutes, and he'll be pleasantly surprised when you tell him the job is done in only 10 minutes! Another mantra:

Try to under-promise and over-deliver, not the other way around!

If you over-promise and under-deliver, you'll quickly lose clients.

4. What items should I *not* bring up with the client?

When you're updating clients throughout the project, remember to keep that same excitement and positivity that you initially had—keep the negatives to yourself. Sometimes issues occur that do *not* need to be brought up to the client because you're able to resolve them internally without affecting the outcome of the job. Sometimes the items you *think* are negatives are items the client will never even notice, so resist the urge to bring these kinds of items up to him. More often than not, he will love your work if you've earned his trust and you are doing everything else right.

For example, if you're striving for excellence on a regular basis, your client will probably not notice that the color you used on her cake frosting wasn't the exact color you intended, or that one of the photos you gave him wasn't the exact shot you were hoping for, or that the meat you served wasn't presented on the plate quite the way you thought it should be. The client will simply love your work because he loves you and trusts you!

If you're really worried that the client will notice one of these items that you can't change, throw in something extra to divert attention away from the issue. If you're an event planner, for example, you could tell the client that you've included a few extra decorations on the head table (perhaps you had a cancelled job, and you didn't want those beautiful decorations to go to waste). Be careful about this—don't do it if you're not sure the client will like the extra decorations, or if those items won't go well with the theme or style of the event.

If a bigger negative issue arises, don't avoid it—you must have a conversation with the client and make it right or fix the problem. Here are some examples:

- You're a photographer and all your client's photos were lost because someone broke into your car and stole your camera.
- You're a dress shop owner and you just learned that a dress you ordered for a client is now on backorder and won't be arriving until after the client's event.
- You're a consultant and you're scheduled to give a seminar on the same day that your mom or your child has been scheduled for emergency surgery.

Obviously, these types of issues cannot be easily resolved, so you'll need to immediately communicate these kinds of issues to the client. In Chapter 7, we'll go over how to address these types of issues and what to do *before* contacting the client about the problem.

5. What else do I need to communicate to the client?

Another topic that applies to the follow-up and updates discussion is information you need from the client to move forward with the project. In my business and in many others, you can't move ahead with a project until the client provides certain information or materials. A florist may need color selections to select flowers for a client party; a video production company may need electronic logos from a corporate client to finish producing a promotional video; a calligrapher may need the final guest list and the correct spelling of each guest's name to complete the escort cards for an event.

Make sure to go through the process of completing the client's job on a written timeline before you get to the point where you need these items, and ask the client for the necessary items much earlier than you need them. The items you'll need should also be outlined in your contractual agreement so the client knows his responsibility to provide these before you start work. Asking the client for items as early as possible will allow you to keep your timeline on track and, by the way, it will also give you another reason to communicate with and update your client during the project, which is always a good thing!

—

In this chapter we've reviewed how to update your client, when to update your client, and what types of items to update the client on. We've also discussed when to contact the client about issues that occur during the project. In the next chapter, we'll talk further about dealing with and resolving customer issues, how to get to the root of the problem, and how to turn those unfortunate problem situations into satisfied customer scenarios.

What are three ways you can start updating your clients during their projects, even when you think you have nothing to tell them?

CHAPTER 7

DEALING WITH (AND RESOLVING) CUSTOMER ISSUES

"Running away from any problem only increases the distance from the solution. The easiest way to escape from the problem is to solve it."
—Unknown author

No one enjoys dealing with customer issues, but in every business, issues will arise. How you deal with these issues is what sets you apart, and dealing with them in the proper way can gain you even more goodwill with your clients. In some cases, handling client issues positively, and in the right way according to the *client*, can forge an even better relationship with her than you had before the issue arose.

Research shows that it costs between 5 to 10 times more—some sources say up to 30 times more!—to acquire a new customer than to retain an existing customer. Clearly, it is extremely important to keep your current customers satisfied.

In this chapter, we'll discuss how to handle and resolve customer issues, look at examples of phrases and questions to use with upset clients, and examine communication methods to use during a crisis situation with a client.

1. Don't avoid client issues.

First, when a client issue comes up, resist the temptation to avoid it. I know it's difficult because most of us do not enjoy confrontation, but if you want to be successful in business, you need to learn to address client issues head on. Avoiding these conflicts will only hurt your business, since you won't achieve resolution with your client, and she will walk away dissatisfied. And believe me, a dissatisfied client will certainly not be referring friends and family to your business if issues are left unresolved.

If you force yourself to think about possible resolutions before having difficult conversations with your client, you'll be more confident and calm in your communication about the issue. This is the first step to actually addressing issues with your clients.

Coming up with possible options to fix the problem in your brain and on paper before presenting them to the client will work wonders. Consider the possible questions or objections your client could have to your solutions before you present them.

Think about the following questions before, during, and after your discussion about the issue with your client:

- What is the *real* issue from your client's perspective? Sometimes clients are angry or they go off on tangents because they are venting frustrations about a problem; let them vent and listen to what they say, but then ask pointed questions to discover the real issue.
- What are your options to deal with the issue? List them out on paper!
- How could the client react to these options? What objections might she have to these options, and how will you address her objections?
- What caused the issue in the first place, and how are you going to address that? How are you going to ensure the problem doesn't occur again, with this client or with others?
- How are you going to rectify the problem? What does the client expect you to do to rectify the problem? You and she may answer this question differently!

- Are there multiple ways to resolve the problem? What are those various resolutions and how are you going to explain them to the client?

- Have you apologized to the client? Always apologize for the problem *and* for the inconvenience to her. However, don't apologize and then do nothing to solve the problem—this is a huge mistake and will only make her more upset.

- Have you followed up with the client after resolving the issue to ensure she's satisfied?

- What are you going to do for the client for her trouble? Perhaps you can offer a gift card to her favorite store or spa, a free product from your company, a discount on her current project, or a free lunch from your company at her favorite restaurant.

These are all questions you need to ask yourself before you consider a client problem as resolved. The last question is a biggie. You always, *always* need to do something for your clients for their trouble, especially if the issue is your fault or your company's fault. Fix the problem at your cost, send the client a gift card as a thank you for her patience while you worked through the issue, or do any of the above suggestions—but *always* do something to make the client feel better, even if she says, "Oh, you don't have to do that."

2. Talk to the client about issues.

Be careful about your method of communication when dealing with client issues. We'll talk more about this in Chapter 8, but when it comes to customer issues, gauge when you need to pick up the phone and have a conversation with the client! Sometimes this is very difficult to do because you may feel afraid to talk to the client since you know she's upset. But remember that ideas and intentions can get entirely misunderstood in emails or texts, so electronic communication can potentially make the situation with your client even worse. Also, once you put something in writing or in email to an upset client, there is now clear documentation of what you said, so it's much better to appease the client by talking with her first. That way, you clearly understand the true nature of the client's issue before trying to resolve it. You often need to *talk* to a client to hear her tone of voice, to let her describe the problem to you, and to truly gauge the seriousness of her issue.

Talking to the client isn't always a bad, frightening thing; we often build up scary situations in our heads so they seem much worse than they actually are. People are much more likely to be reasonable when they have to explain an issue to a person directly, versus "venting" in an email or a text message. We see evidence of this concept every day on the internet and on social media: people will say things about others that they would never say to someone's face. If your Facebook friends were actually talking "live" to certain groups of people, their comments would most certainly be toned down.

So what can you say to your upset client? In addition to thinking about the questions above, here are some phrases you can use with an unhappy client:

- "I'm so sorry to hear about the problem. Let me assure you that we will get to the bottom of this."
- "I'm so sorry about the problem. Just to make sure I fully understand the issue, can you explain to me exactly what happened?"
- "Thank you for explaining everything to me. Again, my sincerest apologies. I understand your frustration. I am going to do x, y, or z to look into this and I promise to get back to you with an update by noontime tomorrow. Does that sound reasonable to you? Is there a better time to reach you tomorrow and is this number the best way to reach you?"

Remember to keep a sense of urgency during this process. It is possible to remain calm about the situation while also making the client feel that solving the problem is your first priority. If the client feels you are doing your best to resolve the matter as quickly as possible, and that you're not avoiding the issue, you might be surprised at how reasonable she seems to become.

3. Anticipate potential issues.

You might even be able to anticipate certain issues before they come up and resolve them before your clients complain. Did you meet your projected timeline, or were you late on the project delivery? Did the client have any issues during the project that you already resolved? Is there something the client *could* complain about, but hasn't yet? Anticipate these issues and do something for your clients to appease them in advance. Even if your clients haven't complained yct, they could complain later to their friends if you haven't gone "above and beyond" for them!

For example, if you were late on your timeline, throw in something extra so the client doesn't even think about complaining about it. If I told a client I would meet a certain timeline but I don't, I often throw in a free copy of their video on disc, or an upgraded Blu-Ray disc copy for them—even if they don't complain. I don't make a big deal of it or make them think I royally screwed up; I just keep it low-key and say I included a little something for them because the project took a bit longer than initially estimated. Again, little things go a very long way!

Here's an example of how I resolved a specific client issue in my business, and the steps I took to resolve it:

We had delivered the final product to one of our clients—and unknowingly had made a mistake. Although we quality-check our product multiple times before it goes out, there was, in fact, an issue with this client's final video, but we never realized the problem until the client told us. This client is very detailed and extremely meticulous, so of all our customers, she was the last client to whom I wanted to deliver a defective video. As soon as she realized there was a problem, she emailed me to let us know. She explained that she simply could not deliver the product to her clientele in the current state, and asked what we could do to fix the problem. Now keep in mind that this completed video had already been reproduced onto nearly 50 discs for our customer's own clientele to view (ugh!). So, what did we do next?

Step #1: I responded to the email as soon as I received it, apologized for the problem, let the client know we would look into it immediately, and told her we would get back to her

ASAP with a resolution.

Step #2: Upon looking into the issue, we immediately realized it was our error. We then talked to the client and explained why the problem had occurred, told her we would fix it, and assured her we would reproduce the 50 discs, at our cost, right away. We then put aside our other projects and prioritized fixing this client's video.

Step #3: Once the video was fixed and re-processed and the new discs were ready, I told the client we would hand-deliver them to her place of business. We didn't merely deliver a new box of discs; we removed all the defective discs from the individual cases, inserted the new ones, and disposed of the old ones. It shouldn't be the client's job to stuff all the cases with new discs, since we made the error! This was my way of doing a little something "extra" for her trouble. While I was stuffing cases with the new discs at the client's office, my client was working at her desk nearby, so after discussing business, we had a long conversation about life in general. I learned more about my client that day than I had known before.

During our conversation, she told me she was very impressed that we resolved the problem so quickly. When she realized there was a problem with the discs, she thought she would have to wait much longer for the replacements. I quickly explained it was our fault, and thus our responsibility to drop everything else and fix this. It was our obligation to "make it right." I told her that if necessary, I would have stayed up all night to make sure the issue was fixed, and that we would have done everything in our power to get those new discs to her as quickly as possible—and I meant it! We built significant goodwill and trust with that client by reacting the way we did.

I can honestly say that my relationship with this client has been transformed since that issue. She clearly trusts our company implicitly to "do the right thing" and to always "make it right," and she shows more warmth towards us than ever before. This customer was guarded and "strictly business" at the start of our working relationship, and now she gives me a big hug every time she sees me! This is clearly an example of how a relationship with a client can actually improve after working through a problem together.

—

Now that we've discussed how to deal with customer issues, how to resolve those issues, what phrases and questions to use, and what communication methods are effective during a crisis situation, we're going to talk a bit more about communication methods. Phone, email, text, Facebook: which method should you use and when? Does it even matter? In Chapter 8, we'll discuss the various communication methods and how to know which method is best to use with your clients.

What are three questions you should ask yourself before trying to resolve a client's issue?

CHAPTER 8

COMMUNICATION METHODS

"Never presume to know a person based on the one dimensional window of the Internet. A soul can't be defined by critics, enemies or broken ties with family or friends. Neither can it be explained by posts or blogs that lack facial expressions, tone or insight into the person's personality and intent. Until people 'get that,' we will forever be a society that thinks 'A Beautiful Mind' was a spy movie and every stranger is really a friend on Facebook."
—Shannon L. Alder, American author

In every client relationship, you'll communicate in multiple ways. In today's world, you can correspond in person, by text, email, phone, Facebook, LinkedIn, Skype, and more. So how do you choose which way to communicate with your customers, and how do you decide which method is best to respond to your client messages?

To start, respond to the client in the way she initially reached out to you. If her initial message was by phone, then respond by phone. And so on.

This does not mean you have to continue communicating in the same method throughout the relationship, but since your client reached out to you in a particular way, give her the courtesy of at least initially responding in the same way. You can then "steer" the client toward the type of communication you need next by asking (via the initial communication method) to set up a phone call or a meeting as appropriate.

However, understand that so many words can get "lost in translation" in a written message. Also, as advanced as technology is, it is inevitably flawed—things can always go wrong. People miss e-mails because they get busy or because the messages get labeled as "spam." In my own personal experience, I've sent emails that went straight to a client's junk folder. Even texts can mysteriously vanish into cyberspace.

A friend of mine ("Diane") recently sent multiple texts to another friend ("Chris") about a party they were planning together, and Chris never responded. It turns out that Chris's phone number was inadvertently blocked in Diane's phone (even though Chris was already in her contact list), so Diane didn't receive any of the text messages Chris was sending back. Until Diane finally called Chris to ask why she wasn't responding to her text messages, Diane had no idea there was a problem with her phone settings! This is a real-life example that demonstrates why we can't completely rely on technology.

We all tend to over-rely on technology because it's easier and quicker than having an actual conversation. But as the previous chapter shows, if you are having an issue with a client, it is imperative to have an actual conversation with her to understand the real issue and to ensure that the issue is truly resolved. In addition, face-to-face conversations will truly allow you to gauge a person's demeanor, tone, and interest level—something you can't always judge correctly through email or text.

Here are some general rules about methods of communication for your business:

Text: Use to set up calls or meetings, express quick thoughts, follow up if you haven't received a response from the client, schedule dates/times, and to alert her if running late for a scheduled meeting.

Email: Use for communications too long for text, or to document pricing and other follow-up items/next steps that need to be recorded. Note: sometimes you may want to send an email to a client, but as you're writing it, you realize you should call and leave a voicemail so you can clearly express your thoughts. There's nothing wrong with that. Recognize when you need to express your thoughts verbally, but don't call the client constantly—respect her time, just as you want your time respected.

Phone call or in-person meeting: Use to address issues with a client, determine how to handle a problem, pre-screen clients (you can use a phone call before setting up a face-to-face meeting as needed), brainstorm about project details, or to get a group of people together who are working on the same project. Skype or some type of online meeting can work for this purpose, too.

When I receive an email inquiry from a potential client, but I know I'll need a phone call to get all the information to develop a proposal, I'll provide some information in the email back to the client (briefly answering the client's questions), but I'll also intentionally leave out some details. I'll save the most important information for my phone call with her.

For example, if the client only asks about price in an email, I often provide general pricing in my reply, but I also explain the factors I use to come up with a specific price for her project (i.e. locations, timing, final deliverable, etc.). That way, the client understands I'll need more information from her before providing an exact price, and it is clear why we need to set up a phone call as a next step.

In many cases, a client's willingness to communicate is actually a good way to pre-screen her. In my business, if a potential client is not willing to talk with me at least briefly over the phone, or to answer a few questions, it typically means she's not the right client for me. In every project I've won, the client has always been willing to have an in-person meeting, or at least a phone call or Skype session, before agreeing to use my services. The potential clients I've communicated with *only* via email have not resulted in "won" business.

If the client wants to meet too soon or insists on an in-person meeting before providing any details about the project, that can be a red flag too. For example, if I agree to meet with a wedding client without knowing any details about the wedding or the budget, I risk wasting an entire afternoon to attend a meeting, only to find out that the client's low budget is never going to match my pricing, no matter how nice she is or how much she wants to work with me. I'd prefer to know that before I waste hours of my time driving to, participating in, and driving back from a meeting with someone who is never going to use my services. This is time I could be using to work on completing other client projects, marketing my business, or on communicating with other clients who are truly interested in my services. Therefore, I pre-screen the client using email and phone prior to setting up a face-to-face meeting.

In some cases, a live meeting is absolutely necessary to determine the needs for a project (e.g. the production of a complex corporate video), but in other cases (e.g. wedding clients or consumers who need to be aware of minimum prices), it's perfectly reasonable to have an initial phone call and then meet later in the process, once you've determined if the client is a good "fit" for you, and vice versa.

Now don't get me wrong—if you currently have no clients or you have no idea what customers are looking for in a service like yours, it may be perfectly reasonable to set up a meeting.

For the purposes of this book, though, I'm assuming you have already figured out what your clients are generally looking for as it relates to your service or product. Think about how much your time is worth, and whether or not other activities are a better use of your time than an in-person meeting, based on the level or stage of your business.

Adjusting to your client's preferred method of communication throughout the project can also be helpful for your relationship. Look for patterns in the times and methods of your client's responses. If you keep reaching out to her by email, but she always messages you through Facebook (perhaps because she's always logged on to her account), try to mirror that communication by messaging back through Facebook. Remember, it's not about you, it's about the client—so try to make life a bit easier for her. If she usually responds to your emails late at night, but doesn't respond during the day, try emailing her at night if you have a question that requires a faster reply. Emailing the client at a time when she typically seems to respond may result in a quicker response time for you.

Some clients will even tell *you* how they want to communicate once they start a project. A client of mine recently introduced herself through Facebook, but once we communicated about her project and established a meeting time, she asked me to contact her in the future through email. She explained that she only checks her Facebook messages at home from a desktop computer once a day, but she checks both her personal and business email throughout the day at work. I told her that was not a problem, but I also asked her to reply to my first email when it arrived so I knew she had received it. I also gave her my email address beforehand so she could add it to her address book, thus not risking a delay in our future communications.

If you use these methods, you'll be able to prioritize your communication tasks each day with your various clients.

—

Now that we've discussed the various communication methods and when to use them, let's talk about getting feedback from your client.

When the project is over or nearing completion, I'm sure you're hoping for a positive review, testimonial, or referral from your customer. How do you get that review? When is the right time to ask for it? What do you need to include in your written message when you ask the client to write one? We'll cover all of this, and more, in Chapter 9.

How are you going to change your use of various communication methods with your clients after reading this chapter?

CHAPTER 9

AFTER THE PROJECT–REVIEWS, REFERRALS, AND FEEDBACK

"88% of customers trust an online customer review as much as a personal referral."

—BrightLocal, SEO reporting and data service, 2014 Local Consumer Review Survey

"Do what you do so well that they will want to see it again and bring their friends."

—Walt Disney, pioneer of the American animation industry

The project is over and you want a positive review from your client, a testimonial to use on your website, or a referral, but you're not sure how to get one from your client. When do you ask, how do you ask, and who do you ask?

In today's online world, you can find reviews on anyone and everyone—big businesses, small businesses, individuals, freelancers, healthcare professionals, and many others. This is exactly why it is so crucial to make sure the information posted about you online is positive! Prospective customers can search the name of your business, and in a matter of seconds, they can decide whether or not they even want to make contact with your company.

1. When is the right time to ask for a review?

Strike while the iron is hot! If you get an email from your client raving about your work after receiving the final product, or telling you how incredibly happy he was after purchasing from you, or commenting on how beautifully everything turned out when you worked together, now is the time to ask! Not only is the client very happy with your product or service, but he's also genuinely excited about the experience with your company in this *exact* moment, so it's the perfect time to ask for the review.

One of my clients recently wrote me this thankful Facebook message, shown below. After responding to it, I sent her a personalized request for an online review, because I already knew she was extremely satisfied with our work:

> Michele and Alan—We have no words that can possibly express the gratitude we have for the absolutely BEAUTIFUL and PERFECT wedding video and highlights montage you both have created! We are both in awe! You were able to capture all the most important parts of our wedding day and there is no favorite part to the video as we LOVE it ALL!!! Please post the highlights video for all of our friends and family to enjoy as much as I know we will for years and years to come!! Thank you from the bottom of our hearts!!!

Now, mind you, you shouldn't simply respond to this type of client message with "Thanks—will you write us a review?" As we've talked about in previous chapters, you should react and respond to what the client has actually said in the positive email or message. Before asking for a review, reconfirm the client's feelings of excitement and confidence in your company by commenting on the items he mentioned he liked best about your product or service.

Here is some sample text you can use when you write back to your happy client:

- "Thank you so much for your kind words and for taking the time to give us such wonderful feedback. I just knew you'd love [pick something he commented on in his message]—it was one of my favorite parts too, and we're so very happy to hear you liked it as much as we did!"
- "I'm so glad to hear your family enjoyed it [or the name of the final product] as much as you did. Thank you so much for taking the time to write—you truly made our day!"
- "Your glowing feedback is so very appreciated. Your kind words truly make all our long hours of hard work so very worthwhile! We can't thank you enough!"

You can ask for the review at the end of this exchange with your client, after you've had a genuine exchange about his positive experience, and after you've reinforced his satisfaction with your company.

2. How do you ask for a review?

If your client hasn't already asked where or how to write you a review, then write him back again, after responding to his initial positive message using the methods outlined above. In the same message or in a follow-up message, if necessary, ask if he would be willing to share his positive feedback online in a review.

Below is an email template I typically use with my clients when asking for a review on an industry-specific review website. I use practically the same words on each request, so I just copy and paste this language into emails for various clients:

Hi _____,

Hope you had a great weekend! You had such an amazing wedding day!

Thank you again for your kind words about your wedding video! Alan and I both greatly appreciate it & hearing feedback like yours truly makes our long hours of hard work so very worthwhile!

When you have a chance, would you mind taking a few minutes to share your positive feedback for us online on The Knot?

If you have a few moments to share your thoughts, it would be so helpful to us and also to other couples who are looking for professional videography services in the future. Sharing either your general thoughts or details about your experience with MPD Video and/or about your favorite parts of your wedding video would be great. If you prefer, you can just copy and paste the email you wrote to me after you received your video, to make it easier on yourself. I've pasted the text from your email below for your reference:

Michele and Alan - We have no words that can possibly express the gratitude we have for the absolutely BEAUTIFUL and PERFECT wedding video and highlights montage you both have created! We are both in awe! You were able to capture all the most important parts of our wedding day and there is no favorite part to the video as we LOVE it ALL!!! Please post the highlights video for all of our friends and family to enjoy as much as I know we will for years and years to come!! Thank you from the bottom of our hearts!!!

You do need to sign in to The Knot to post a review, but it only takes a few minutes to sign in or to set up an account. Below is the review link for you if you'd be willing to say a few words:

https://www.theknot.com/review-wedding-vendors/ mpd-video-productions-whitinsville-ma-375501

Thanks so much in advance for your help, and for choosing us to capture your special day.

Have a great week & congrats again to you and _____ [insert name of spouse]! We hope you enjoy watching the video and re-living your beautiful wedding day for many years to come!

All our best,

Michele & Alan Fleury

MPD Video Productions

Note the following elements in this email:

- Respect for the client's time: I make sure to tell him it only takes a few minutes of time to write a review.
- Ideas on what to write: Make it easy on your client! In this case, I even provided the text from the original positive email message I received from him, so he doesn't even have to think about what to write.
- Reason why it's important for the client to write a review: It's not for you, necessarily, but to help others who are also "in his shoes," looking for the same product or service.
- Easily accessible review link: All the client has to do is click on the link we provided to submit his review.
- Sincere thanks, thanks, and more thanks for the positive feedback!
- An incentive or "thank you gift" can also be included as needed: In some cases, I offer a free extra copy of the video or a gift card as an incentive, particularly if I want the review to be posted by a certain date, and I always mail out the gift the same week the client meets my deadline.

So what do you do if the client hasn't sent you a raving email about your product or service? What if you think you did a great job, but you're not sure how to get his feedback? In this case, give the client a reason to get back in touch with you. Ask him to reconnect with you *after* you know he's received the final product.

In my case, when I send a client the final video, I write a key statement in my final email, or in a letter or note included in the package, asking the client to get back in touch with me about a particular topic. With a wedding video, I might write:

- "We can't wait to hear how you liked re-living your special day and which parts of the video you liked seeing the best—please let us know!"
- "Once you and your husband get a chance to watch the complete video, let me know and I'd be happy to post your highlights video online for your friends and family to view. We can't wait to post it for you, but we wanted to make sure that the two of you see it together before we share it with the world!"

With a corporate video, I may know that the video will be used at a particular meeting or event, so I'll ask the client to let me know how everyone liked the video at the meeting. The last time I did this, I received the most touching voicemail from a corporate client, telling me how happy he was with our work and how he was simply amazed at the great reaction the video received!

I also try to be as personal as I can, where it makes sense to do so. With a wedding client, I may write a personal note congratulating the couple and commenting on a part of their wedding that I loved, and then I include some candy or microwave popcorn with a note that says, "Enjoy the show!" This personal touch goes a long way.

With a graduation client, I may include a small gift with an inspirational quote on it like, "Every day is a new adventure!" or "Live the life of your dreams." You can find inexpensive gifts like plaques, mugs, or journals at places like TJ Maxx, Michael's, or on clearance racks at various stores the end of the season.

3. Who do you ask for a review?

Of course you can always ask your primary contact with any project for a review, but it's not just the direct customer who can provide you with a review or a referral—keep indirect customers in mind as well. Maybe your direct client is a mom, but the indirect customers are her kids, husband, or mother. Maybe you hit it off with one of those indirect customers, or one of them had a particular liking for your work. You can ask all these indirect clients for reviews as well. I have received reviews in the past that "count" online as three separate reviews, but each review is actually from a separate person involved in the same project with me. What an added bonus!

Even if you're unable to get a written review, try to make note of positive comments that your clients or your indirect customers make throughout the course of the project. These quotes can be used on your website or as testimonials in the future, so jot them down for future use!

Also, don't forget to remind your customers about the possibility of referring you to others, but be realistic about it. Just because a client's best friend could need your services for an upcoming event—and this is the first thing you think of when you see her Facebook post about it—this doesn't mean that *you* are on the client's mind, and understandably so. Your client and her friend are likely preoccupied with the initial planning of this event. You may be tempted to ask if the friend needs your services, but just subtly offer your help or assistance. Give your client a quick reminder that you are there to help if she and her friend need it—don't "pounce" and try to push your services on them. Have you ever known someone like that? The pushy salesperson who happens to be a friend of your husband's, or the multi-level marketing person you try to avoid when you see him approaching in the grocery store? Who wants to do business with someone like that? No one!

Just let people know you're there if they need you, and offer your advice and assistance where you can. I've seen realtors put this extremely effective quote at the bottom of every email they write:

"The best compliment I can receive from my clients is a referral to their friends and family."

What a great reminder to keep that real estate agent in mind in the future, right?

—

In this chapter, we've provided some tried-and-true techniques for asking clients for reviews, how to determine the right time to ask, and suggestions on who can provide those reviews for you. Now that you have some great reviews, testimonials, and referrals, you're on your way to building a stellar online reputation that will lead more and more customers your way in the future. Remember, people trust the advice of their friends, and they trust input from real people who have bought similar products and services, so positive reviews are an excellent way to attract new clients!

What are three ways you can ask your clients to give you positive feedback after the project ends?

I hope you've found the ideas, tips, and techniques throughout this book helpful for you and your business. Now you are ready to start winning (and wowing!) new clients, and you are armed with a multitude of tips and techniques that will turn those clients into happy customers! I look forward to sharing many more ideas and tips in the future, because this book only reaches the "tip of the iceberg" of topics from my many years of working with all types of clients.

In my Companion Workbook, I've included reference materials and additional resources that can help you implement the techniques discussed in this book within your own business. Many of the questions and processes I've described in this book are outlined in the Companion Workbook, so you can easily use them with your own clients. You can download the workbook here:

https://whattheydontteachyouinbusinessschool.lpages.co/freeworkbook/

Thank you for reading! If you enjoyed the tips in this book and are willing to write a review on Amazon, I would be very grateful. It only takes a few minutes...thank you in advance!

ABOUT THE AUTHOR

Michele Fleury is a graduate of Boston College, where she graduated with honors with Bachelor's degrees in both Marketing and Economics. She has over 25 years of successful experience in sales, marketing, client service, and account management. Michele has worked in a variety of industries including high-tech, travel, relocation, and retail, in the areas of business development, account management, and project management. Michele's extensive client-facing experience has provided her with a deep understanding of what business owners, salespeople, and service agents need to do to effectively sell their products and services, and to provide stellar customer service in a highly competitive environment.

After many years working in the corporate world, Michele began to develop a strong desire to leave the "corporate grind" and wanted to start her own business. In 2007, she and her husband founded MPD Video Productions, an award-winning video production company providing video services to all types of clients including individuals and families, engaged couples, small businesses, large corporations, dance studios, theater groups, and more. Upon entering the small business arena, Michele quickly realized how many business owners lack critical sales and service skills, and how strongly this deficiency and inability to work with clients affects the success of their businesses. Michele felt compelled to share her vast sales and service knowledge with the world, in order to help other businesspeople with techniques on selling and servicing prospects and customers, communicating and setting expectations with clients, and building customer loyalty.

Michele has a love of working with customers and thrives on providing a positive experience for all her clients. She lives in Massachusetts with her husband Alan.

ACKNOWLEDGMENTS

There were so many amazing people who inspired me and supported me in writing this book:

My accountability partner, Mary Cheyne -- without you, this book truly would not have been possible. Your constant weekly support and your drive inspired me to finally finish this book, and I cannot thank you enough. I consider myself so lucky to have met you through this book-writing process, and I've gained a lifelong friendship that I will cherish forever.

My editor, Elayne Wells Harmer -- you are so much more than an editor! Your insights, recommendations, and abilities were invaluable. Your warmth and excitement during this process made me feel like I had a trusted friend working with me. I hope we have the opportunity to meet someday, and I look forward to working with you on more books in the future.

My cover designer and formatter, Vanessa Mendozzi -- you

are such a pleasure to work with! Your creativity, patience, and desire to please your clients is an inspiration to me. I love the book cover you designed for me!

The program that helped me complete the book-writing process, Self-Publishing School -- without your program, this book (and so many others!) would never have been written or published. Thank you for creating a truly priceless program and a proven process for first-time authors to follow.

My friends, clients, and fellow SPS members, who gave incredible advice along the way -- your input was greatly appreciated!

And last, but certainly not least, my husband Alan -- your patience with me on a daily basis does not go unnoticed! Without your love, advice and support, this book would never have been completed. You are my world.

Thanks so much to each and every one of you for your help with this book!

Urgent Plea!

Thank you for downloading my book! I really appreciate all of your feedback, and I love hearing what you have to say.

I need your input to make the next version even better.

Please leave me a helpful REVIEW on Amazon.

Thanks so much!

Michele Fleury

Made in the USA
Middletown, DE
15 July 2017